T0129293

UNKNOWN
Journey
AHEAD

UNKNOWN Journey AHEAD

ANASTASIA NITSIS

iUniverse

UNKNOWN JOURNEY AHEAD

Copyright © 2019 Anastasia Nitsis.

All rights reserved. No part of this book may be used or reproduced by any means, graphic, electronic, or mechanical, including photocopying, recording, taping or by any information storage retrieval system without the written permission of the author except in the case of brief quotations embodied in critical articles and reviews.

iUniverse books may be ordered through booksellers or by contacting:

iUniverse
1663 Liberty Drive
Bloomington, IN 47403
www.iuniverse.com
1-800-Authors (1-800-288-4677)

Because of the dynamic nature of the Internet, any web addresses or links contained in this book may have changed since publication and may no longer be valid. The views expressed in this work are solely those of the author and do not necessarily reflect the views of the publisher, and the publisher hereby disclaims any responsibility for them.

Any people depicted in stock imagery provided by Getty Images are models, and such images are being used for illustrative purposes only. Certain stock imagery © Getty Images.

ISBN: 978-1-5320-7845-3 (sc)
ISBN: 978-1-5320-7847-7 (e)

Print information available on the last page.

iUniverse rev. date: 07/15/2019

Dear Dad,

Even though you are in Heaven now, I know you are you are always watching over me. I want to thank you for being my "hospital buddy" all those years, for ALWAYS being there when I needed you and for being the BEST dad in the world!!!!!

Love and miss you very much!
Soula

This book is dedicated to Nick Nitsis, Dora Daley and all my family and friends that left this earth much earlier than they should have due to cancer.

Chapter One

The summer of 1982 was coming to an end and a new school year was about to start. I felt both excited and scared about entering the 7th grade. This was my first year attending junior high school, and the building was much bigger than the elementary school I had attended the last seven years. In the spring, my sixth grade class had taken a field trip to visit the junior high school, and we were given a tour of the school. I was a little overwhelmed and knew it would take some time getting acclimated to a new school.

The school year started and as I had expected I got lost several times trying to find my classes. After the first week, however, I was more familiar with everything and was able to get to my classes on time. The first month went pretty quickly. I liked my new teachers and my classes, plus I had made many new friends. The one thing I did not enjoy, having to wake up much earlier to get ready for school.

Around this time was when the tiredness began. At first, I just thought my body was trying to get used to the new school year (getting up earlier, walking around a bigger school, more classes than I had before and more homework). I always tried to do well in school and get good grades, although it was never easy for me. It always took me at least a couple of hours to get my homework done, and I studied in my room where there were no distractions. I also was in the habit of getting my homework done as soon as I got home from school, but now I had to take a nap before starting it. I remember trying to stay awake on the school bus on the ride home and, once I got there, just wanting to lie down on my bed for a while. Even when the half hour naps were becoming hour naps, I still thought my body was trying to get use to my first year in junior high school. My mom did not realize I was napping so much because she was used to me being in my room trying to get my homework done.

October arrived, and I was not paying as much attention to the tiredness because I was distracted with my older sister getting engaged. A wedding date was not set, but they were thinking about getting married in September of 1983. My family is Greek, so my sister would have a big fat Greek wedding. Even though an official wedding date had not been set, my sister and I began going to different department stores to look at dresses. We had a lot of fun!! Also, Halloween was coming, and I always loved getting dressed up in costume for Halloween. This year, however, since I was in junior high, I thought I was too old to go Trick-or-Treating. Instead, decided I would pass out candy now. But when Halloween night arrived, I did not feel very well. My stomach was upset, and I had a headache so I ended up lying on the couch most of the night. My mom felt bad for me because she knew how much I enjoyed Halloween. She checked on me frequently during the night, but I did not have a fever and I was not vomiting so she was hoping it was just a "24 hour bug".

Even though the tiredness and occasional headaches continued, again I did not pay too much attention to the symptoms because I was more focused on going shopping for wedding dresses with my sister. I was really excited about getting to order my dress because I was a bride's maid for the first time rather than a flower girl. I was also preoccupied with the approach of Thanksgiving and Christmas. I always enjoyed these holidays. I loved going over to my aunt's house (my mom's sister who I called Thea Katina. "Thea" is the Greek word for aunt) for Thanksgiving. Then, usually the day after, me, my sister Ellen and my brother Jimmy, would spend the day decorating the Christmas tree and putting up the Christmas lights. I had a lot of fun decorating the tree and putting up Christmas decorations. Before I knew it Thanksgiving and Christmas came and went.

The New Year began, 1983, and I was doing well in my first year of junior high. Before I knew it January was over. In February my sister found out she was pregnant so the "September" wedding was going to have to be moved up a few months. My parents were not too happy about this since it gave them less time to get things ready for a Greek wedding. Plus, they were going to be grandparents sooner than they had expected. For me, this was GREAT news. I was going to be an aunt, and I was going to get to wear the pretty bride's maid dress sooner than I thought. I was almost thirteen and the only things I had to worry about at that the time were doing good in school, hair, makeup, clothes and boys. So for me, becoming an aunt seemed very exciting!!!

Around the second week in February I became sick again with some kind of stomach flu, similar to what I had during Halloween, but this time it was worse. Unlike the "24hr" bug I had before, this time, I missed four days of school which did not make me happy. I knew I would probably get behind in my classes and I would have a lot of homework to make up. I recovered from that illness too and to my surprise I did not fall too far behind in my classes.

March was approaching and I was eagerly anticipated about my birthday coming up. Even though I still was not feeling 100 percent, I just continued not to pay too much attention. Then one morning while I was getting ready for school, I noticed some bright red spots on my arms. They were not bumps but red dots about the size of a pinhead, and they were under my skin. Since they did not itch or hurt, I did not show them or mention them to my parents. My birthday party was in a few days and I did not want them to cancel it because I was sick. Also, I thought they had enough things to worry about right now with the wedding and all. When I got on the school bus that morning, I showed the dots to my friend to see what she thought, wondering if she had seen anything like this before. She told me she hadn't and that if they got worse I should show my arms to my parents. The spots went away after a couple of days and with my birthday, I forgot about the red spots. But then, a couple of weeks later the red spot came back, but this time they were on my legs. Still, not wanting to worry them, I chose not to say anything to my parents.

March was almost over and the school's third quarter was coming to an end. Even though I had exams during the week, it was a fun time at school. I was looking forward to the longer weekend since it was Easter weekend. Little did I know that I would not be returning back to school for that last quarter.

Chapter Two

Easter Sunday

I woke up not feeling well. Of course I had to feel sick on Easter Sunday!! So much for eating all kinds of candy like I usually did on Easter, I thought. I told my mom "I don't feel so good today. I feel really tired, my stomach hurts, I'm dizzy when I stand up and I think I have a fever." "Come here" said my mom, "let me feel your forehead." My mom could always tell by feeling my forehead if I had a fever. "You do feel pretty hot. Why don't you have some toast and a little juice and then I will give you some Tylenol." My mom did not like to give me medicine on an empty stomach. "Okay mom, I will try to eat something, but I don't know if it will stay down" I told her. I ate a little bit of breakfast and then she gave me some Tylenol. "Go lie down for a while" mom said, "hopefully, you will feel better when you get up."

I fell asleep for a couple of hours but I did not feel any better when I got up. Jimmy thought it was funny to tease me with our Easter baskets and eat his candy in front of me, but mom said "quit teasing your sister, she does not feel good." My mom took my temperature again, and I still had a fever. She had me eat a little bit of lunch and gave me some more Tylenol and told me to go lie down again. I had slept most of the day, and my fever was not going away, I still had an upset stomach and I was getting a bad headache. I really could not remember a time when I felt this bad.

My parents became concerned. Instead of me feeling better as the day progressed, I felt worse. My dad came over to me "hey honey, are you still feeling pretty bad?" I responded "yeah dad, I do. You know I don't complain about feeling sick, and I would never ask to go to see a doctor unless I felt really bad. I know it is Easter, but do you think the Urgent Care Center up the street is open?" My dad knew I must be feeling awful to be asking to go see a doctor. "We can try the Urgent care first, if they are not open I will take you to the ER at the hospital, okay?" My dad told my mom, "I'm going to take Soula to the Urgent Care first (my Greek nickname is Soula). If it is not open I will take her to the ER at St. George Hospital. We will probably be gone for a couple of hours." From past experience of having three children and having to take us to the doctors, my dad knew we would be gone for a while. My dad and I kissed my mom goodbye and he told her "I call you if we are later than two hours."

On the way to the Urgent Care I was hoping it would be open. I knew it would probably be a shorter wait to see the doctor there than going to the ER and, as bad as I felt, I did not wish to sit in a "waiting area" too long. Pulling into the parking lot we could tell the Urgent Care was open because the lights were all on and the "OPEN" sign was lit up. My dad and I walked in, and I was glad to see that there was only one other person checked in ahead of us.

The receptionist called us to the window as soon as we walked in. My dad told her he brought me to see the doctor because I was feeling so sick. She started asking me a bunch of questions and I told her how bad I had been feeling all day. I also told her about the tiredness I'd been experiencing for a few months, the headaches, and the red spots that had shown up on my arms and legs. I could tell by the look on my dad's face that he was not very happy with me not mentioning any of this to him or my mom. He said "why didn't you tell me or your mother about this stuff going on." I told him I did not think it was anything serious and I did not want to worry them. "You should have told us" he scolded me.

We did not have to wait long to be put in a room. The nurse called my name to "come on back." She was very nice and friendly and said "so you are not feeling so good today? I'm sorry you feel so sick on Easter." She asked what symptoms I had, and repeated to her what I told the receptionist. "Okay, sweetheart, I am going to take your vital signs before the doctor comes in to see you." My temperature was at 101F, not sure what the rest of my vitals were. The doctor then entered the room and introduced himself. "Hello Mr. Nitsis and Anastasia, I am Dr. Brown." He was very nice and friendly too. He had a smaller build, dark hair, wore glasses. My dad was much taller than he was. Dr. Brown went over all the symptoms I had been having over the last few months. Then he asked my dad "would you mind if Anastasia changed into a gown so I could do a thorough examination on her?" Dad said "that is fine, I'll go out to the waiting room while she changes." I was thirteen so my dad knew I would be a little embarrassed changing in front of him. I was given a gown and Dr. Brown and the nurse stated they would give me a few minutes to change then they would return to my room. Dr. Brown and the nurse returned and when he started to examine me, he noticed numerous bruises on my body that I had no idea were there, especially since they were on my back and other places that I would not be able to see without using a mirror. Use of a mirror for me at that time was: fix my hair, put on makeup and make sure the clothes I had on looked good. He asked me where I got all these bruises from. I told him I did not know I had them, nor did I know how I got them. Concerned with the bruising, fever, and the other symptoms I had within the last few months Dr. Brown told my dad he wanted to draw some blood from me and perform some blood tests to see if there was anything abnormal. My dad asked me "are you okay with them taking some blood from you? They are going to have to poke a needle in your arm to get the blood." I told my dad "yes, I am fine with that, as long as it helps to find out why I feel so bad!"

After Dr. Brown was done drawing the blood from my arm, he gave me some gauze and told me to hold it in the spot where the needle was. "I'll be back in a few minutes," he said. My dad also got up to leave the room and stated he was going to the restroom. I waited and waited for what seemed like forever and still no sign of either my dad or the doctor. While I was waiting I was thinking to myself "I hope there isn't something too seriously wrong with me since it is taking them so long to come back to the room."

Then, I saw my dad walking past my exam room, and he is vomiting into a pink emesis basin. At this point I really start to worry and thought to myself "this is not good, why does Dad look so pale and why is he getting sick!" Dr. Brown finally came back to my room and told me that he was concerned about some of the test results and that there was an ambulance already at the Urgent Care. I was going to be taken to Children's Hospital right away. The doctor would not give me any more information than that. I asked Dr. Brown where my dad was and he said he would go get him.

My dad and the paramedics entered the room at the same time. As they were getting me onto the stretcher, I asked my dad "why am I going to Children's Hospital?" "I'm not sure", he replied. Only it turned out he did. During the long wait when I was wondering what was going on, Dr. Brown spoke with my dad. Dr. Brown explained to Dad that with the symptoms I had for the last few months and the blood test results, he suspected the possibility that I had Leukemia. This was why I needed to be taken to Children's Hospital immediately. With my dad being in a state of shock, Dr. Brown thought it would be best for me to be transported to the hospital by ambulance rather than my dad trying to drive me.

Also, during that wait my dad called home, hoping my sister would answer the phone. Luckily she did and my father told Ellen what was going on and if she could drive my mom to the hospital, but not to tell her exactly what was going on so she would not be hysterical on the way to the hospital.

While the paramedics were getting me comfortable and secured on the stretcher I asked, "is it okay for my dad to ride in the ambulance with me? I'm really scared about going to the hospital and I would like my dad with me." Both the paramedics, a lady and a man, were very nice. They were trying to make me as comfortable as I could be on the stretcher. The lady replied, "yes, your dad is coming with us. However, he will be riding in the front of the ambulance, he can't be back here with you. Is that okay?' I started to cry, "yes, that's okay. I just want my dad with me."

As the paramedics were putting me in the back of the ambulance I overheard them talking and saying "I hope that is not what she has." I had never been in an ambulance before and the paramedics knew how scared I was. To keep my mind occupied with good thoughts, they asked me all kinds of questions. "Where do you go to school?" "This is my first year at Gamble Junior High." I told them about the different classes I had and talked about some of my teachers. "Do you have any brothers or sisters?" "I have an older sister Ellen, she is getting married soon and she going to have a baby too. I am very excited to be a bridesmaid in her wedding and to becoming an aunt too! I also have a younger brother, Jimmy. We are only a year apart so we fight a lot, but I guess all brothers and sisters do." I answered their questions the best I could, but at one point I let out a big scream. "Are you sure we are safe back here and we are not going to fall out the back doors! The doors are locked!" Riding in the back of the ambulance, up and down the hills of Cincinnati, felt like I was on a roller coaster ride!! The paramedics responded "yes we are safe, we travel up and down these roads all the time. We know it feels a little scary back here but we are okay." After a long ride, at least it felt like it to me, we arrived at Children's Hospital.

Chapter Three

At the hospital there were four doctors already waiting for us and I was put in an exam room right away. Still not sure why I was taken to the hospital, I could tell by the look on my dad's face that it was not good. The paramedics transferred me from the stretcher to a wheelchair that was in the room. They said good-bye to us and told me "we hope you feel better." Then the one of the doctors in the room asked my dad "with the possibility that she has Leukemia we would like to draw some more blood and do a few more tests of our own to go along with the blood test results we received from the Urgent Care." LEUKEMIA, DID I JUST HEAR THE DOCTOR SAY LEUKEMIA!!! I thought to myself "How can this be? Yeah I have been feeling a little sick these last few months, but come on, Leukemia!! I just don't believe it!!"

Before I could ask the doctors any questions I was wheeled down to the lab area so the lab technicians could draw some more blood. It only took a few minutes for them to get the blood vials that they needed filled and I was wheeled back to the exam room.

While I was down at the lab area, my mom, sister and soon to be brother-in-law arrived at the hospital and joined my dad in the exam room. While I was out of the room the doctors told my parents and my sister they were pretty sure I had Leukemia. They broke down crying because they automatically thought it meant I was going to die. We had watched a movie recently called "Something for Joey". It was a true story about a boy who was diagnosed with Leukemia in the early '70's and did not survive. The doctors told them if I had been diagnosed 10 years earlier, I would not survive. But, because of research in the last few years, survival rate of this type of Leukemia (ALL) had significantly improved.

As I entered the room I could tell they were crying and they were trying to wipe the tears from their eyes so they would not get me upset. Now with me back in the room and both my parents present, the doctors introduced themselves. "Hi, I am doctor Alex." Dr. Alex had dark short hair, a little short, and wore glasses. "Hi, I am doctor Peter." Dr. Peter was tall and thin, had red hair. "Hi, I am doctor Jerry. I will be one of the doctors involved in Anastasia's care while she is an inpatient and I will be her doctor when she comes to the outpatient oncology clinic." Dr. Jerry was about my dad's height, had brown hair, also wore glasses. "Hi, I am doctor Kathy. I will also see Anastasia at times in the outpatient clinic." Doctor Kathy was pretty, had a soft voice, long brown hair. All the doctors were very nice and tried their best to explain why they thought I was feeling so sick. They stated that with the blood test results they received, the increased tiredness, headaches, bruising, and the red spots under my skin (which are called petechiae), they believed that these were all signs and symptoms of Leukemia.

There were so many questions in my head I did not know what to ask, plus, I did not want to upset my parents with more "not so good" information. I did ask them, however, if I would be out of the hospital for my sister's wedding which was in about seven weeks. I told them how excited I was about her wedding and that I was going to be one of her bride's maids. The doctors said they thought I should be discharged from the hospital by then, but, due to the chemotherapy I would probably be wearing a wig by then. OKAY...BACKUP FOR A MINUTE...I WAS GOING TO LOSE MY HAIR!!!

I asked "what do you mean I'll be wearing a wig by then." Dr. Alex proceeded to tell me that due to the strong chemotherapy drugs I would be given in the next few weeks I would lose all my hair!! That was when I started to cry. Up until then I was taking the information the doctors were telling me pretty good. But being told I was going have to go through all this "crap" and lose my hair, I just broke down and cried!!

I could not believe what they were telling me, that I was going to be bald within a few weeks. I was thirteen, didn't they know how important appearance was at this age. Plus, how could I look pretty at my sister's wedding if I was bald!! All the feelings of excitement I had for her wedding were shattered!!

The doctors try to calm me down and tell me the hair loss was temporary and it would grow back, but it did not make me feel any better.

By this time it was almost midnight and we were all getting tired. Dr. Jerry thought it would be best to go over more information in the morning. My parents were told that there was not a room ready for me since it was so late but there would be one ready for me sometime tomorrow. For tonight, I would be taken up to the Neonatal ICU. Before I went upstairs Dr. Alex stated he wanted to put an IV in my hand so that the ICU nurse could administer some IV fluids that were going to be ordered. Even though it hurt a little he had the IV in quick. Then he was taping it down and taping my hand to a special board to keep my hand straight so not to kink the IV line. I had to say good-bye to my sister and "brother-in-law" at this time since only my parents were allowed to go to the Neonatal ICU with me. Ellen gave me a big hug as she tried to hold back her tears, "I love you and I will see you tomorrow. Try to get some sleep, okay." I gave her a big hug also, "I love you too!"

Dr. Peter and Dr. Kathy said good-bye to my parents and me and stated they would see me again after I was admitted into a room tomorrow. Dr. Alex and Dr. Jerry took us up to the ICU. In the elevator I look at my parents, and they look bad. They look like the life has been sucked out of them. I know all the thoughts going on in my head; I can only imagine what is going on in theirs'. They had just been told their daughter has cancer and she may die. Even though I was the one with this grim diagnosis, I was worried about my mom and dad. We got to the ICU and there was a hospital bed already there for me. The doctors said "goodnight" to us and stated they would be back around 9:00AM. They also told us to try and get some sleep, "yeah, like that was going to happen", I told myself.

The nurses and my parents got me settled, and my nurse for the night got the IV tubing, IV pole and pump all hooked it up to me and began administering the fluids. She told me the fluids might feel a little cold at first but if I felt any burning in my hand to let her know. I was also hooked up to some other monitors that were in the ICU. My parents made sure I was comfortable in the bed before they had to leave. I could tell by the look on their faces that they were worried about leaving me alone for the night. They gave me a big hug and kiss and told me "see you in the morning." I knew they were trying their hardest not to cry but I could see the tears in their eyes.

After my parents left I looked at all the equipment I was hooked up to. I looked at the IV in my arm and thought this was all a horrible dream. I did not get much sleep that night. I had so many thoughts going through my head. Up to this point of my life I was a healthy kid. I had the occasional cold or the flu a couple of times, but for the most part I was healthy. I thought to myself "How can I have Leukemia? How can I have cancer? Am I going to die? Do I have the strength to go through all the tests and chemotherapy treatments the doctors talked about?" At this point, wondering what the future held, I started to cry again. I did not cry too loud, I did not want the nurses to hear me. Again I thought "how can I have cancer? I am scared! I am afraid of dying!!!" With all those fears in my head the night proved to be a long one. I tried to fall asleep but sleep would not come. In addition to all that was going on in my head it was hard trying to sleep in the ICU with all the noise from the machines and monitors. Plus the room was not very dark so the nurses could see while they were working. I probably got one hour of sleep (at the most) that night.

Chapter Four

Morning came and my spirits rose when my parents arrived. "Did you get any sleep?" my mom asked. "Yes," I lied. Not wanting them to worry that I was up all night. I could tell that they had not slept much either. Dr. Alex and Dr. Jerry arrived, and I started to feel very nervous. They tried to explain to me and my parents what a bone marrow aspiration/biopsy was. Dr. Alex stated "A bone marrow test is done on a part of the pelvic bone. A hollow needle is inserted into the pelvic bone so we can aspirate (pull out) some bone marrow. The reason we need to perform the bone marrow test is so we can examine the blood and marrow cells and confirm the diagnosis of ALL Leukemia." Dr. Jerry said "I will be the one performing the test. I will tell you step by step what I'm about to do, and do my best to keep you comfortable during the procedure. You will still feel some pain, however, because even though the skin where the needle is going in will be numbed, the bone cannot be numbed." Great!! That just made the knots in my stomach feel so much better!! They asked me if I was ready to go to the treatment room, and I told them "No, but I don't think I'll ever feel ready so I might as well just get it over with."

I was taken by wheelchair from the ICU to a treatment room. We entered the treatment room and it was not what I expected. The walls were bright and colorful, I guess since it was a Children's hospital the rooms were more "cheerful" than a regular hospital. Dr. Jerry told me to get on the treatment table and lie on my stomach. He told me to try and relax as much as possible (easy for him to say) because the more relaxed I was the less pain I would feel. I tried to relax and lie still so he could get started. Dr. Jerry told me the first thing he was going to do was clean the area of my lower back where the needle was going to be inserted. "You'll feel some coldness on your back, okay."

He waited a few minutes to let the solution dry before injecting the numbing medicine. Then Dr. Jerry told me, "Take a deep breath while the numbing medicine is injected. You are going to feel a burning/stinging as the numbing medicine goes in, and breathing in may decrease the burn." Boy, he wasn't kidding, even with taking a deep breath it still really burned!! At least the burning did not last too long. Then I was told the needle was going in, and that I would feel some pressure and some pain but to keep trying to relax. I tried to be strong and not cry but I couldn't help it. It really hurt!! Not only could I feel the needle going into the bone but I could feel it coming out too!! Dr. Jerry apologized for hurting me, "Anastasia, I am so sorry. I know the test is painful, but we need to get your bone marrow so we treat you." "I'll be okay, just give me a few minutes," I told him.

After the bandages were put on I was told that I would experience soreness in my lower back for a couple of days, but the nurses would give me Tylenol to decrease the pain. I was taken back to the ICU where my parents were waiting for me. "You've been crying," my mom said. "Are you alright?" my dad asked with a worried look. "I tried so hard to be strong not cry during the bone marrow aspiration. I didn't want you and mom to worry so much about me, but I couldn't help it, it just hurt too much." Even though I was the one going through all the painful tests, I could see the pain my parents were feeling. Seeing the tears in their eyes after each test I had gone through, I knew they were hurting just as much as I was.

While I was gone my parents were told a room was ready for me on the third floor. I was only back in the ICU for a few minutes before there was a "transporter" there to take us to my room. I told the ICU nurses good-bye and off we were. We got to the room, and for the most part I liked it. I had never been admitted into a hospital before so I really didn't know if it was a good room or not. Just like the treatment room, this room was colorful and different pictures hanging on the walls. I looked around: there was the hospital bed, a couch, a bathroom with a toilet and shower, and across from the hospital bed was a mirror and sink. There was also a small closet to put my personal belongings. The nurses and my parents helped get me situated in the room.

A short while later, Dr. Jerry (the doctor that performed the bone marrow aspiration) entered the room. "Hello Mr. and Mrs. Nitsis. Hi Anastasia, are you okay?" "My back is sore but I'll be okay" I told him. "I hate to tell you this, but, there is one more test I need to perform. I need to do, a spinal tap." Dr. Jerry stated that it would be a little painful like the previous test. "For this test, I will numb an area of your back near the spinal column. A needle will be inserted between the vertebrae so I can collect some spinal fluid. The spinal fluid is needed, along with the bone marrow sample I got earlier, to confirm the Leukemia diagnosis. The bone marrow and spinal fluid are also needed to decide the type of chemotherapy treatments that would be best for you."

Once again the fear began to rise inside me. I no longer believed him when he said "it will only hurt a little." I was wheeled down to the treatment room for the spinal tap to be done. Again the uneasy feeling I had in my stomach returned. I was told to lie on the treatment table, only this time he wanted me to lie on my side with my back towards him. One of the nurses from the outpatient clinic entered the room. "Hi Anastasia, I am Emily. I will be assisting Dr. Jerry with the spinal tap. You can hold my hand if you want to." "Yeah, I would like to hold your hand. The numbing medicine really burns when it first goes in!" Emily could see the scared look on my face. She rubbed my shoulders and said kindly, "you can squeeze as hard as you want to, okay." Then Dr. Jerry asked me to get in a fetal position. "I need you to hold your knees as close to your head as you can." Emily helped position me on the table. He stated, "I need you to be in this position to help open the space between the vertebrae, otherwise, I can't insert the needle into the spinal column and collect the spinal fluid that is needed."

"Okay Anastasia, I'm going to get started" he said. I felt the coldness of the iodine and then the burning of the numbing medicine. I squeezed Emily's hand like she told me I could until the "burning" went away. Dr. Jerry told me I needed to be very still and not move while the needle was being inserted. Even though this did not hurt as bad as the bone marrow biopsy, I could feel the pressure of the needle going into my spine. I had to lie there for a few minutes while he waited for the spinal fluid to drip out into the test tube. Even though I was lying very still, inside I was shaking like a leaf!! When he obtained the amount of spinal fluid that was needed he told me the needle was being pulled out and to remain still. I could feel him remove the needle but it did not hurt too much and I just waited for him to tell me I could move again. I was bandaged up once again and told to sit up slowly. Dr. Jerry had me sit for a few minutes before getting off the table and back into the wheelchair. I told Emily, "Thank you. Holding your hand made me feel better during the test. I hope I didn't hurt your hand." "No honey, not at all. Glad I was able to help." Emily was very nice and I hoped I would see her again the next time I had to get a bone marrow or spinal tap done. As I was taken back to my room I still was in disbelief that I had Leukemia. I thought if this was just the beginning of the kind of stuff I would be going through, I hoped I had the strength to keep on going.

After a while all the test results were in and the "team" of doctors that would be caring for me came to my room. Dr. Alex began, "As we had suspected, Anastasia has ALL Leukemia. We were hoping it was ALL since it is the most curable of the childhood Leukemias." "We plan on," said Dr. Peter, "Anastasia being in the hospital around two weeks for her induction phase of chemotherapy." Dr. Jerry continued, "As we mentioned before, the chemotherapy will be administered in different methods. During this Induction phase, the plan if for Anastasia to receive Vincristine by vein, L-asparaginase by injection into the muscle (IM),

Methotrexate into the spinal column (because ALL Leukemia cells collect in the lining of the spinal cord and if not treated, they could cause a relapse of the Leukemia), and Prednisone by mouth." Dr. Alex stated, "The goal of the chemotherapy is to kill the cancer cells and put Anastasia into remission, a state where the Leukemia cells are no longer seen in the blood or bone marrow. To achieve this, however, there are going to be side effects of chemotherapy." "We know for sure," said Dr. Peter, "That she will lose her hair and a decrease in her immune system would occur. Other side effects that may also occur are: anemia, infection, mouth ulcers, diarrhea/constipation, nausea/vomiting, and tiredness."

My parents, and me, tried to take the information in as best as we could. We all were in shock of the diagnosis. Confused, my dad asked, "How did she get Leukemia when she is such a healthy kid. Was it something we did or did not do? Could we have prevented this from happening?" Dr. Alex responded, "We do not know exactly how Anastasia acquired the Leukemia. Mr. and Mrs. Nitsis, you are not responsible for her getting cancer. You both have to accept that you did not cause Anastasia to become ill." The doctors continually stated to us that me being diagnosed with Leukemia was not my parents or my fault.

Then my mom asked about me returning back to school, "You said before, that she was going to be in the hospital for at least two weeks. What about her going back to school?" "We are uncertain of when Anastasia will be going back to school," said Dr. Jerry. "Our main focus right now is getting her Leukemia in remission. We have a teacher here at the hospital to help the kids with their school work so they don't get behind. I will have her come and visit with you later today if that is okay. She will take care of contacting Anastasia's teachers and getting assignments, alright?"

"That is fine," said my dad. "Anastasia's sister, Ellen, is at her school right now letting her principal and teachers know she is in the hospital." Dr. Jerry continued, "We know there is still two months left of school before summer break, however, it is possible that Anastasia will miss the remainder of the school year. Even if we are able to get her in remission and she is discharged from the hospital before school ends, her immune system will be very low and we do not want to take the chance of her getting an infection while attending school. The doctors did not know what the days/weeks ahead would bring but they stated they would do their best to get me into remission and feeling better.

Then Dr. Alex asked, "Anastasia, do you have any questions for us?" I asked about the chemo treatments I was going to get and he repeated the information to me. Then I asked again, "I am going to lose my hair FOR SURE because of the chemotherapy. There is NO WAY that I will be keeping my hair?" Dr. Alex said, "I am so sorry but, the chemo you will be getting WILL make your hair fall out. It will probably take two to three weeks before your hair starts to fall out, but it WILL fall out. However, in a couple of months your hair will start to go back even though you will still be on chemo."

Hearing Dr. Alex confirm that I WOULD lose my hair made me cry again. My mom and dad hugged me and told me "it's going to be okay honey." I just hugged them tight until I finally stopped crying.

My parents followed the doctors out into the hallway as they were leaving. Dr. Peter stated he would be back in a little while with some booklets that had information about ALL Leukemia that seemed to be helpful for parents.

I could not see my mom and dad out in the hallway, but I could hear them. I heard my mom telling my dad "why are they saying so much stuff in front of her?" (When I was first diagnosed, my mom was not too happy that the doctors were so open and honest with the information about Leukemia in front of me). "She is only thirteen; she is too young to be told that she might die." "Don't they know that all this stuff is scaring her?" Then she said "why is this happening" as she started to cry. I could tell my dad was crying, too. I was the one diagnosed with cancer, yet I realized this was harder for my mom and dad to deal with.

Parents try so hard to protect their children from things that may cause them harm, injury or pain. In this situation, however, they had to let the painful things happen to me in order for me to survive and this was very difficult for them to accept. When they came back into the room they apologized to me, they said they did not want to get me upset with their crying. I told them they had nothing to apologize for. Their daughter was just diagnosed with cancer; they had every right to cry! I hugged and kissed them both and told them how much I loved them. "I know I am very sick and that the days ahead will not be easy", I said, "but I am going to be strong and do what I have to do to get better." We all hugged again wiping our tears away, "it's going to be okay, we are going to get through this", dad said.

My sister Ellen and brother Jimmy arrived at the hospital not long after this. My dad asked Ellen, "Did you go to Soula's school to let them know she is in the hospital?" "Yes," Ellen said, "I went to her school. I spoke to the staff in the main office and with her principal." Of course the staff and my principal were shocked to hear I was in the hospital for being diagnosed with Leukemia. My principal told Ellen, "I'll let all her teachers know why she is absent and if they have any assignments for her. Call me back next week and let me know how she is doing. Tell your sister we are thinking about her and hope she gets better."

My mom and dad then asked Jimmy how he was doing and how his school day went. Jimmy did not have much to say. He was more worried about me being diagnosed with Leukemia. I was a year older than Jimmy. Being so close in age we fought a lot like brothers and sisters do, but me being sick changed things. He was being nice to me and truly concerned about how I was doing. I'm sure like everyone else in my family, including me, he was wondering if I was going die.

As we were talking about school, the nurse entered the room and stated there was a school teacher that worked at the hospital to help kids get their school work done while they are in the hospital. "I'll call Mrs. Smith, the teacher, and give her Anastasia's name," said the nurse, "once I call her she should be in contact with you in a day or two." The next day, too soon for me, Mrs. Smith did come to my room to get all the information she needed about where I attended school and the name(s) of my principal and teachers. Within a week, Mrs. Smith had received English and Math assignments. My principal told her, as long as I completed the assignments for those two subjects that would be fine. I was hoping that being in the hospital I would not have any school work, but that was not the case!

Chapter Five

My Thea Katina, who is my mom's sister, and my cousins, Christine and Souli also came to visit me. I could tell that, while my mom and aunt were talking, both of them were in "disbelief" that I had been diagnosed with cancer. My cousins looked like they were in "shock", too. My parents and my sister told them everything the doctors had said and that I would be in the hospital for a least two weeks. I did not know what "life" was going to be like having cancer, but I was very thankful to have my family there to help me get through it!! My aunt and cousins did not stay too long because they knew I had a long day. They hugged and kissed me "good-bye", "we'll see you soon" they said.

As my second night in the hospital approached, I felt very tired. With all the tests throughout the day and not sleeping too much the night before, I was ready to go to bed. While my mom and dad were helping me get ready, I knew mom would be staying the night with me. My parents had discussed who would stay during the night with me before they had come to the hospital that morning. My mom said she wanted to stay with me the first night. For the next seven weeks, except for a few times, my parents alternated staying the night with me so I would not be alone. Even though I was thirteen and old enough to be by myself, I was really glad to have my mom or dad with me during the night.

I climbed into bed and gave my sister, my brother and my dad a big hug and kiss and said "goodnight". My dad, Ellen and Jimmy said "we love you and we will see you tomorrow." I told them, "I love you too." My dad told me "Try and get some sleep tonight, okay." "I will try my best", I told him. My parents said goodnight and goodbye to each other and I could tell this had been a long and hard day for them too. Then my dad, Ellen and Jimmy left my mom and me for the night.

Despite being tired, I still could not get to sleep that night either. Too many thoughts were going on in my head for me to fall into a deep sleep. Again I thought about being diagnosed with cancer and still could not believe it. I felt very afraid of the unknown journey ahead. No one in my family had a life-threatening illness before, so I had no idea what to expect. Even though we did not attend church on an every Sunday basis, I had always believed in God. I said prayers, but not every night. That night, however, I prayed. "God I'm afraid and I really need your help right now. I pray that I will go into remission. I will do whatever I need to do (chemotherapy, painful tests) to get better. Please God, I am only thirteen; I am too young to die; just help me get better!" I continued to say my prayers every night after that before going to sleep.

Morning arrived, and I could see that my mom did not get much sleep either. I knew from that point on not only was my life about to change, but so was my family's. I just hoped we all had the strength and courage to get through this. My "induction" was successful; however, I had numerous complications during my seven week stay in the hospital. I knew that I had a difficult journey ahead of me but I had no idea how difficult it was going to be.

Chapter Six

The first week in the hospital proved to be overwhelming: all the doctors in and out to see me, the tests, daily blood draws, and more. At the time when I was diagnosed, central lines that are used today for patients were not very popular. I had to have a new IV put in every 72 hours. This was not enjoyable, especially being in the hospital for seven weeks. By the end of my hospital stay, my doctors were scratching their heads trying to figure out where to put the next IV! And with the daily blood work, there were times I tried to pretend I was asleep so the lab techs would leave me alone and maybe not take my blood. But, that did not work. There were times the sun wasn't even up yet, and they were at my bedside poking my arm!

Nighttime was not much better. The nurses came into the room on a regular basis, noise coming from the machines that were in the room, and having to go to the bathroom while dragging the IV pole behind me. (When you are getting IV fluids pumped into you 24/7, there is no sleeping through the night without trips to the bathroom!).

Plus, I was still trying to grasp the fact that I had Leukemia. I kept thinking to myself "how could this be?" It still did not seem real.

I had many visitors (family and friends) stop in to see me the first week in the hospital. I was very glad they came to visit and help me keep my mind off being diagnosed with cancer. My cousin Chris attended classes at University of Cincinnati. The university was a few minutes away from the hospital. She said she could come visit me regularly, which she did.

In the beginning of my hospitalization, other than the induction for chemotherapy, the main concern my doctors had was the anemia I developed. This was the reason I felt so tired since the beginning of the school year. I was given numerous blood and platelet transfusions to help increase my blood counts.

This was the time when AIDS and HIV were first publicized on TV. As blood was being infused into my veins, news reporters were warning the public about this new deadly disease called "AIDS" and that it could be contracted by receiving "blood products" that had the HIV virus in them. My cousin Chris was visiting at the time. I looked over at Chris and she could see the worried look on my face! I asked "Do I have to worry about getting AIDS now? It's not enough to think about dying because I have cancer. Now I have to worry about dying because of getting "bad" blood too!!" Chris tried to calm me down but I knew she was worried, too. "Soula, don't get worked up. Right now just focus on getting better. I'm sure the doctors will be talking to you and your mom and dad if there is something to worry about." We tried to talk to my nurse about what the media stated on TV about AIDS. My nurse would not tell us much. She said I had to wait until my parents and my doctors were present to get more information.

Now, not only was there a concern about my anemia, but the huge concern about me getting HIV from the blood products I recently received. The doctors tried their best to calm my mom and dad's worries about the blood transfusions and told them that any future blood products I would receive would be thoroughly tested for HIV before they would be used. My parents didn't know what to believe and they just tried their best not to look too worried or upset around me.

Not only for me, but for many people, this was a really scary time because so many people depended on blood products to survive. I was very lucky that none of the blood products I received had the HIV virus. However, I developed fevers and bad chills when I was given the transfusions. My mom and dad would worry so much when they would see me shaking so bad even though I was covered with blankets. I was hoping that would be all the "bad" stuff I was going to have to deal with during my hospitalization and by the next week I would be going home. WRONG-THINK AGAIN!!!

It did not take long, since my immune system was decreased from the chemotherapy, for me to get an infection. This would be the first of several "isolations" I would have to deal with. Before entering my room, visitors had to wash their hands and wear a mask. I developed a streptococcus pneumonia infection which was initially treated with penicillin. I had not been allergic to penicillin before but this time I had a severe allergic reaction and broke out with very bad hives.

I was covered from head to toe with a bright red rash. The rash was so bad that several doctors came to look at me because they were not sure at first what was wrong with me, I felt like some kind of alien. The doctors decided to take a skin biopsy from my right thigh to determine what was causing the rash. To this day you can see the circular scars on my thigh.

The test results came back and my parents and I were told the rash was caused by the penicillin and that another antibiotic would be given to me. The rash made me itchy from head to toe, I felt so miserable. The nurses gave me Benadryl and some other anti-itch meds but they did not help relieve the itching that much.

With my immune system being low, I was told not to scratch my skin because the doctors were afraid of me getting another infection. But I was so itchy. Knowing how miserable I felt, my mom came up with the idea of using the long Q-tips that the hospital had to "softly" scratch my body. The doctors said that would be okay as long as we did not press down too hard on my skin. This helped a little bit with the itching, but not as good as my fingernails.

After about a week the rash started to go away. However, because the rash was so bad my skin began peeling. Again, the doctors were worried about infection so I was told to be very careful when showering and not to rub hard on my skin and accidentally cause an open tear of the skin. The doctors told me to let the skin fall off and not to try and "peel" the dead skin off.

As the second week was coming to an end I knew I wasn't going home. The rash was healing but not gone. It took one more week for the rash to heal completely.

Chapter Seven

The third week started worse than I expected. Not only was I beginning to lose my hair, I was starting to develop mouth ulcers and sores on my lips too!

I remember waking up one morning and noticed some strands of hair on my pillow. I started to cry. Ellen stayed with me that night to give my parents a break. When she woke to me crying, she flew off the couch and came to my bedside. She thought I was in pain since I was crying. "Soula, are you okay? What's wrong?" I told her I wasn't in any pain, I was crying because my hair was starting to fall out. "Look at my pillow Ellen. See all the hair that's on it? I'm really going to lose my hair!!" I thought maybe the doctors were going to be wrong about me losing my hair, but they were right!!! I can't lose my hair! I don't want to be bald!!!"

I took the comb from the bedside table and ran it through my hair. A big clump of hair was in the comb and seeing that made me cry harder. Even though it was the least painful physically, losing my hair was the hardest to deal with emotionally. Ellen hugged me, she did not like seeing me so upset. I could tell it bothered her too that my hair was falling out. "Soula, it is going to be okay. Let me have the comb, try to comb your hair gently like this. I know your hair will still be falling out, but not as bad if you don't comb it so hard." Ellen helped me get dressed and fix my hair so not too much hair fell out. She tried her hardest to make me feel better, but she knew it was going to take some time for me to get used to being bald.

Since it was the third week, I had hoped the doctors were wrong about me losing my hair. The reality hit me like a ton of bricks. "Ellen," I said, "thanks for helping me get dressed and making me feel better. I'm glad you were able to stay the night with me last night." "You are welcome," she said, "anything for my sister. I know it is going to be hard losing your hair but I will help you through this. Together, we can come with some cool ideas for some hats or scarfs for you to wear, okay." "Thanks again Ellen, I love you" I said while hugging her. "I love you too," she replied, hugging me even tighter!

Also, as my doctors' predicted, I started to get mouth ulcers due to the chemo treatments. Lucky me, not only were there ulcers in my mouth, I got sores on my lips too!! The ulcers and sores got so bad that I could only eat with my front teeth. I could not open my mouth like I wanted to, nor could I chew my food. As a result, it would take me about two hours to eat a meal. By the time I was done with breakfast, the lunch tray would arrive. By the time I was done with lunch, the dinner tray would arrive. Between the mouth ulcers and the chemotherapy altering the taste of the food, eating became more of a chore. I tried my best to eat what I could but food was no longer enjoyable. My parents, my sister and other family members brought me different foods they thought I would enjoy but I just wasn't able to eat them.

I remember Ellen brought me a fudge popsicle (which I loved prior to getting the mouth ulcers) and it was a disaster. I could barely open my mouth to even taste it and then it just started to melt all over. I was so frustrated I started to cry because I really wanted to eat it.

Because eating became so difficult for me, I lost 20 pounds while in the hospital. I went from 90 pounds at admission to 70 pounds when I was discharged. Also, because of the ulcers, I was unable to brush my teeth with a tooth brush. I had to clean my mouth with a hydrogen peroxide and saline water solution and use the "sponges on a stick" after each meal and at bedtime. Even though I did not swallow the solution, it tasted horrible. I dreaded whenever I had to rinse my mouth. The mouth ulcers lasted about three months so I did not start to gain any weight back until several months after I was discharged.

By the end of the third week, any hope of going home had flown out the window. Luckily, I had my family and close friends who came to visit me regularly. They helped keep my mind off of not going home yet.

Chapter Eight

Since my cousin Chris had classes at University of Cincinnati Monday through Friday, she tried to visit me every day. She was always making me laugh. I was close to my cousin Chris and I was glad she was able to spend so much time with me while I was in the hospital. We had lots of fun times and she was able to stay with me a few nights to give my parents a break.

One night she stayed with me, she brought her "boom box" radio so we could listen to some music. Chris told me to get permission from the nurse before we played anything, she did not want me to get in trouble. When my nurse came by I asked, "Stacey, is it okay if Chris and I turn on the radio? She brought her "boom box" so we could listen to some music. We won't play it too loud, I promise!" "Sure," she replied, "as long as the music is not loud."

At this time, I was not in "isolation" so I was able to keep the door to my room open. We turned the radio on. The music was not loud but little by little, other kids that were patients on the floor too were at my door entrance.

"Can we join you," they asked. "Sure," Chris and I told them, "The more the merrier."

Before we knew it we had a little "party" going on at my room and we were having fun singing and dancing. Seeing how much fun we were having (on a pediatric oncology floor, you usually did not see any "fun" stuff going on), the nurses said we could turn the music up a little. What a fun night! Not only did I need to have a little fun, so did the other patients!

Another event I was looking forward to was my sister's bridal shower. Ellen told my doctors about her bridal shower. She asked them if it would be possible for me to get a "pass" to leave the hospital for a few hours to attend. My doctors said that it could be arranged, but they would not know until the day of the shower. It all depended on how my blood counts were for that day before they could make that decision. Just the small chance of getting out of the hospital, even for just a few hours, was great news to me.

The day of the bridal shower I learned that my blood counts were good enough to leave the hospital for a few hours. Dr. Alex came to my room after getting the test results. "Good morning Anastasia, I have some good news for you. Your blood counts are high enough for you to get out of here for a little while. However, you need to be VERY careful not to pick up any bad germs that could make you very sick. So, while you travel to and from the hospital and while in the room with all the guests, you need to make sure you have a surgical mask on. The last thing we need is for you to contract an illnesses or infection while you are out. Okay?" "I promise Dr. Alex, I will have a mask on," I replied with a big smile on face. I was so excited to be able to go.

"Believe me, I do not want to get any sicker than I already am!!!" Seeing how excited I was he had a smile on his face too. "Alright young lady, have fun today. Your nurse Susan will give you any other info you need before leaving. I'll see you tomorrow." "Bye Dr. Alex, thanks again."

Ellen came to the hospital that morning to help me get ready since my mom was at my aunt's house getting things set up for the shower. After I was dressed, my sister helped me fix my hair. At this time it was very thin from falling out and there wasn't much she could do with it. I had just enough hair left to put a couple of barrettes in to make my hair look somewhat okay. When I was ready, my nurse unhooked me from the IV tubing and flushed the IV. She said I had to be back in six hours so the chemotherapy could be restarted again. My nurse gave me some instructions/precautions for while I was out and then gave me the "okay" to leave. I was so glad to get out of the hospital even if it was for a few hours.

We arrived at my aunt's house to find most of the guests already there. So before I got out of the car Ellen told me to put the surgical mask on so when we entered the house I would be protected. We walked through the front door and the house was full of my family and friends. They were glad to see I was able to attend. My mom hugged and kissed me. She looked pretty in her dress but I could see the worried look in her eyes. I was asked many times "how are you feeling" and I told them I had my good days and bad days. I was just hoping to be discharged from the hospital sometime soon.

I was really glad to see my aunt and my cousins Chris and Souli. Since being diagnosed I was not able to see Souli that much. She was only nine at the time, so she could not come and visit me anytime she wanted to like Chris could. Souli and I were very close and I really missed her. Prior to getting sick I was always over my aunt's house. We were always listening to music. We were either jumping around trying to do "gymnastics routines" or just dancing around to the music. I'm sure we drove my aunt crazy at times because she could never get us to sit still!

I was so glad to be at Ellen's shower. I really needed to get out of the hospital for a little while and spend time with family and friends. After we ate, not that I was able to eat much with the mouth ulcers, my sister began opening her gifts. I felt so happy for her, and I wished I could have helped her out more with the shower and wedding plans. After about half an hour of my sister opening gifts, I began to feel tired. My mom could tell I was looking sleepy and asked me if I was feeling okay. I told her I was just tired and needed to lay down for a little bit. I asked Ellen if she was okay with me resting a while as she continued to open her gifts. She told me that was fine and she was not upset at all. She was more concerned about my health than me watching her open gifts.

I asked Souli if we could go to her room so I could rest for a while. She said "sure." This was only the second time I got to see Souli since I was admitted. I told her I really missed her and I was glad to spend some time just the two of us. We went to her room for me to rest. It was quiet there compared to downstairs where everyone else was. We talked for a little while. She told me how she missed me too and did not like seeing me so sick. "We always have so much fun together", she said, "why did this have to happen?" She hoped I would get better soon and be able to come home.

I guess I was pretty tired because I fell asleep. I woke up to my mom rubbing my head and asking me how I was feeling. I told her I felt okay, just tired. She asked me if I wanted to say goodbye to everyone before they left. I told her I did so she helped me get my shoes back on and re-fix my hair so I looked somewhat presentable. I said goodbye to everyone and told them I looked forward to seeing them soon at the wedding. After most of the guest had left, my mom told me my dad was on his way over to my aunt's house with my brother Jimmy. They wanted to spend some time with me before I had to go back to the hospital.

Dad and Jimmy arrived and they asked how I was feeling. I told them I felt okay with the usual tiredness. My mom and my sister helped my aunt clean up and my dad helped get my sister's gifts in the car. After a while my dad noticed it was time to go back to the hospital. He asked me if I was ready. "No," I replied, although I knew I had to go back. I told my dad even though I was only out for a few hours it was nice to get a break from being in the hospital. I said goodbye to my mom, sister, and brother and told them I loved them and would see them tomorrow. I said goodbye to my aunt and my cousins and told them I hoped to see them soon.

On our way back to the hospital my dad asked me how the shower went and if I had a good time. I told him "I think it went well, I'm not 100% sure because I had to lie down for a little bit. I did enjoy being able to get out of the hospital and to seeing everyone for a while."

When my dad and I returned to the hospital we went straight to the nurses' station so my nurse would know I was back. Within a few minutes she was in my room with IV bags and hung them on the IV pole. I asked her if she could wait a couple of minutes so I could change into my pajamas before hooking me back up. It was so much easier to get clothes on and off when you're not hooked up to an IV. She said that was fine and helped me get changed. Then, once again, I had chemo running through my veins.

Chapter Nine

Now, week four, doctors told us that I had developed temporary diabetes due to one of the chemotherapy drugs I was on, L-Asparaginase. During my induction, I was receiving IM injections of L-Asparaginase. The injections were given in my upper thighs, and I was given one each week. I was supposed to receive nine of them in all. Due to developing the diabetes, my doctors decided not to give me the final dose.

My nurses were checking my sugar levels with urine glucose sticks and injecting me with insulin (either in my arms or legs) twice a day. Since my doctors were not sure if I would still have diabetes when discharged from the hospital, they wanted my nurses to teach me how use the urine glucose sticks and give myself insulin injections. I told the nurses, "I don't mind learning how to use the glucose sticks but there is no way I was going to give myself insulin injections!!!" I had no problem for someone else to giving me a shot, but I could not give one to myself! My nurses wanted me to at least try and practice. They brought me oranges, apples, pillows and even a cloth doll to try and practice on but I just could not inject myself. Luckily, as it turned out, by the time I was discharged I no longer had diabetes.

End of week four, things continue to get worse. Because my platelet count was still a little low, I developed bloody stools. Once again I was given blood and platelet transfusions, however, I continued to have blood in my stools.

Since the doctors were not sure if the bleeding was coming from my stomach, they wanted check the contents of my stomach. So, a couple of nurses entered my room and stated they needed to put this tube (which they showed me) up my nose and then guide it down my throat and then into my stomach so they could remove some contents to see if there was any blood in it. "There is NO WAY you are putting that tube up my nose," I told them. "Can't you just put the tube down my throat," I asked. "We cannot put the tube down your throat because you would gag too much. Putting the tube up through your nose and then guide it down the back of your throat, helps with the gag reflex."

I started to panic and cry because I knew this was not going to feel very good. The nurses tried to calm me down and told me it was really important for them to do this procedure. I told them "okay" but to go slow. They agreed and began putting the tube up my nose. I started to freak out because it was hurting and told them to pull it out. One of the nurses said "let's try again and try to relax." They lubricated the tube again and tried a second time. Lubricated or not, having a tube shoved up your nose does not feel good!!

Little by little they were getting the tube past my nose and down my throat. I started to panic again because I was gagging as the tube was going down my throat. One of the nurses got me a glass of water and told me to take some small sips as the tube was going down to help with the "gag reflex". Finally, they got the tube into my stomach and then took a big syringe and suctioned some fluid out. After they collected what they needed, they told me to take a few breaths and relax while they pull the tube out. Well that did not help because the back of my throat and my nose really burned as the tube was being pulled out. I hope I NEVER have to have that done again in my life because it was very unpleasant!!

Even though the "gastric contents" that were tested showed the bleeding was not coming from my stomach, the doctors wanted an ultrasound of my abdominal area done to make sure. An ultra sound was done and confirmed the bleeding was not coming from my stomach. The doctors stated it was possible that the bleeding might be coming from the rectal area. They said what might have happened, with my platelet count being so low, just passing a stool caused a major bleed to occur. I was given numerous transfusions of platelets and packed red blood cells. I also remember the doctors were very worried that if they could not get the bleeding to stop that they might lose me. I did not find out until years later how serious the bleeding was and that I almost did not survive. My dad told me the doctors confronted him about how they were trying everything they could to stop the bleeding. My doctors were running out of options. My dad told the doctors "do whatever you have to do to save her life." I do not know what my doctors decided to do to stop the bleeding, but it took about three weeks before the blood in my stools had stopped.

Week five. After being in the hospital for over a month, I thought I would never go home! One thing after another kept happening and it just seemed like my life would never be normal again. When I looked in the mirror, I recognized less and less of myself. I would see this thin, bald, sick person looking back and I would cry. I felt so sick, and when things kept going from bad to worse it was really hard to keep a positive attitude.

There were many days that I did not feel well and did not think I had the energy to keep fighting. My family and friends, however, told me giving up was not an option. They were constantly doing things to keep my spirits up. I was lucky to have the love and support that I received from my family and friends. I would not have been able to get through this without them. My family did so much for me and made so many sacrifices. I know the doctors were the ones that gave me the chemotherapy that got me into remission, but I also needed that support. Otherwise, I do not think I would be here today!

Chapter Ten

Since I had been in the outpatient clinic for the bone marrow and spinal tap tests the nurses in the clinic were getting to know me. I guess they could tell I was a little depressed. So, when one of the Leukemia patients that had been it remission for a couple of years came to the clinic for one of her checkups, they asked her if she would mind visiting me to help cheer me up a little. I was watching TV when she came to my room. She told me who she was and asked if she could visit with me for a while. I was very glad to see her. Up to now, even though there were other patients on the floor, they were a lot younger than me. So, I really did not have anyone to really talk to about how I was feeling. The girl told me she had finished chemotherapy (after two years) about two months prior. To see her, she did not look like she was in remission for Leukemia.

She was pretty, did not appear to be sick at all and she had a full head of hair! I asked her how the past two years of being on chemotherapy had been and how did it feel now that she was done with treatments. She told me a lot of stuff, some good and some not so good but I was glad to talk to someone who knew what I was going through. I told her how I felt and how when I looked at myself in the mirror I thought things were never going to be normal again. Looking at her so healthy and with beautiful hair I only hoped that one day I would have a "normal" life again. She told me each person has their own experience with cancer and how things turned out for her may not be exactly how things would turn out for me but to keep a positive attitude and keep fighting. I was very glad she came to visit me, because she gave me hope and some very good information.

Now it was week six, more fun to come. I was washing my hands and noticed a hard blister on my right thumb near the thumb nail. I showed it to the doctors when they came to my room during "rounds". They looked concerned and one of the doctors said he would be back in a little while. As promised, the doctor returned and had a small syringe and needle to get some fluid out of the blister. I was surprised that it did not hurt too much. He said he would come back later once he got the test results back.

As I mentioned earlier, eating no longer was not enjoyable. My mom and dad tried their hardest to bring me food that they thought was soft enough to eat and tasted good. My mom brought me some of her homemade chicken and rice soup, hoping I would be able to eat that. This soup had always been one of my favorites. She warmed some up for me and put it on the table in front of me. It looked and smelled good and when I tried a small spoonful, to my surprise it tasted good too. It had been a while since something I ate (due to the chemotherapy and mouth sores) actually tasted good.

I had been eating the soup for about 20 minutes. Most people would have finished the soup by now, but I was still eating because of the mouth sores. Then, the doctor that did the test on my thumb returned to my room. He told my mom and I that the test results showed the blister was an infection, and that he needed to drain the rest of the fluid out of the blister. I asked him if it was going to hurt and he told me he was going to numb my thumb so it wasn't going to hurt too much (like I haven't heard that before!). My mom asked the doctor if he could come back in a little bit since she just gave me some soup. The doctor told my mom it wasn't going to take long, "just let me get this done quick, and then she can go back to eating." My mom was reluctant but she let him proceed anyway.

As usual, the "it won't hurt too much" was incorrect because it hurt like hell!!! The doctor kept sticking me with this big needle that had the numbing medicine in it six or seven times. This really hurt!! Why numbing medicine has to sting so badly, I don't know. I started to cry which really made my mom upset. As he was draining the blister, the doctor informed us that he was going to cut my thumb nail off too. The blister was so close to the thumb nail, he was afraid the infection might have gone under the nail. I started to freak out. I thought "how bad is that going to hurt!" The doctor stated since my thumb was already numb, I would not feel him take the nail off. He was right on that one but, I could not watch.

By the time he was done, me and my mom were upset. He tried to comfort me while he was wrapping my thumb in bandages, but I was not in the mood. I guess neither was my mom. My mom was so mad she really let the doctor have it. I was shocked. I had never seen this side of her before. She would get upset with us from time to time when we misbehaved, but she never really "yelled". I guess she was really angry, because when the doctor tried to apologize to her, she told him she did not what hear it. She also said a few "not so nice Greek words" that the doctor did not understand. Go mom!! Even though I was no longer in the mood to eat the rest of my mom's soup, I did anyway. After what I just witnessed, I thought I should at least try my best to make my mom happy again.

With my right thumb nail gone, I had to be very careful not to get another infection in my finger while it was healing. For the next three months I had to soak my thumb in a hydrogen peroxide solution, apply antibiotic ointment and then wrap my thumb with gauze dressing four times a day. What a pain that was!!

Chapter Eleven

During the sixth week, more of my hair began falling out. My dad asked me if I was interested in getting a wig, especially with my sister's wedding coming up. He thought I might like a wig, instead of just a scarf on my head. Even though I was not too thrilled about getting a wig I told him I would like to get one. The nurses told my dad about a local wig company that would bring samples to the hospital and help me pick one and get fitted. I told my dad to make an appointment for them to come to the hospital.

On the day the sales representatives from the wig store came, I was not feeling well physically or emotionally. They were really nice and tried their hardest to show me wigs they thought would look best on me. I, however, hated them all. None of them looked like my real hair did. I think I had an "attitude" because I was upset about losing my hair, and knew that in about a week I was going to be totally bald!. I was thirteen, and at this age hair meant a lot and mine was being taken away from me!

After a while, my dad was getting a little upset with my "attitude". Dad, was really understanding with my mood swings because he knew I had been through a lot of hard stuff. This time, however, he let me have it! "I know you have been through a lot these past few weeks and I know you are upset about losing your hair, but you should not be taking it out on these nice people," he said. "They are only trying to help you find a wig that will look good on you. They know that no wig is going to look exactly like your real hair but they are trying their best. You need to apologize to them for acting like a brat!"

I did apologize and after a while I finally made a decision on a wig. They put the wig on my head and took some measurements so it would fit right. They said they would return in a few days with the finished wig. Dad and I thanked them for coming, and I told them again I was sorry for how I was acting earlier.

When the wig was delivered I had mixed emotions. I liked how the wig looked, but I was still upset about losing my hair. The sales reps asked me to put it on to see if it fit okay. It was hard for me to put the wig on, and when I looked in the mirror I hated it! I did not look like myself. Everyone thought the wig looked good except for me. It was not my real hair and no matter what wig I would have chosen, I would not have liked it.

I only had it on for few minutes, then took it off and set it on the table next to my bed. They gave me information on how to care for the wig, plus a business card so I could call them if I had any questions. The nurses and doctors that came into my room that day noticed the wig on the bedside table. They asked me why I wasn't wearing it and I would tell them "because it's itchy and I don't like it." My sister got there that day before my parents did and she too asked why I wasn't wearing the wig. I started to cry and told her "because I hate it, that's why!" She gave me a big hug and told me she knew I was upset about losing my hair but in a few months my hair would start going back again. I told her "I know, it's just going to take me a few days to get used to wearing it. Don't say anything to mom and dad because I know they paid a lot of money for the wig." When my parents arrived a little later I put the wig on so they could see how it looked. They both thought it looked good and asked me how I liked it. I told them it was nice but it was going to take some time getting use to wearing it.

While my parents were in my room talking with me and trying to get me to eat some dinner, Ellen slipped out of the room without me noticing. She knew I was feeling depressed due to the long hospital stay and all the things I had gone through. So, she asked some of the nurses if she could have a little party for me to lift my spirits up. Ellen told the nurses she would bring in my brides maid dress to see how it fit, especially since I had lost so much weight. While I was in my dress, they could have the "party". My nurses had also noticed some depression and thought this was a great idea. When Ellen returned to my room she noticed I was occupied with trying to eat dinner. This gave her a chance to tell my mom and dad about the party. My parents thought it was a good idea too.

The next day, Ellen came into my room with my bridesmaid dress. My face lit up with a big smile, "my dress, why did bring it here," I asked. Ellen replied, "I know you haven't tried it on in a while so I wanted to see how it fit. Let me help you get it on and maybe you can show the nurses your dress." While my sister was helping me get the dress on, the nurses were getting the "party" set up in the kitchen area. As I slipped into the dress, I could see the worried look on my sister's face because of how thin I was. Ellen didn't say anything she just helped me get into the dress. With hesitance, I put my wig on so my sister could see how it looked with the dress.

We went out of my room into the hallway to show the nurses. As we approached the nurses' station, some of the nurses noticed me in my dress. They told me how pretty I looked, with my wig too. Then one of the nurses told me to go into the kitchen area to show one of the doctors. When I entered the room I got a big "SURPRISE" yelled out to me from several doctors and nurses. On the table were cookies and cupcakes and some Kool-Aid. They said the party was for me to help cheer me up and to keep hanging in there. They knew I had a hell of a hospital stay so far but they had a feeling things were going to get better. The doctors and nurses were telling jokes to make me laugh and get my mind off of having cancer for a little while. One of the doctors even joked "man those slippers are really cool, I bet the other brides maids will be jealous when they see you walk down the aisle with those on!" We all laughed. I had a great time and was glad that Ellen did this for me! I really needed it! I thanked everyone for the party and told them it did help me feel better.

Another event that helped me feel better that week was getting a "pass" to leave the hospital again. As I had mentioned, my family is Greek. Ellen would be married in our Greek church. Ellen had been baptized, however, my future brother-in-law had not. He needed to be baptized in order for them to be married in the Greek Orthodox church. Our church did perform ceremonies for adults that needed to be baptized. I was very glad to get out of the hospital, even if it was for short while, to watch the ceremony.

We entered the church. Even though I physically I did not feel very good, spiritually, I felt really good. Because I was in the hospital, it had been a long time since I was in church. The Father of our church, however, did visit me every week in the hospital so he could say a prayer for me and give me communion. He was very glad to see me at church with my family. I looked around the church since it had been a while since I was there. I always thought our Greek church was very beautiful. My mom and dad helped walk me down the aisle. I was glad to see all my family. My aunt, Thea Katina, and my cousins Chris and Souli were there too. I sat down in one of the pews while everyone was getting things set up for the baptism. Sitting there, I closed my eyes and said a prayer. I prayed to God again that he would help me get better.

The ceremony did not last too long, and there were some funny moments. I was really glad I was able to leave the hospital for a while and spend time with my family and have a few laughs. Before we left the church our Father said a prayer for me and gave me communion again. My parents and I thanked him again for the prayers and for visiting me in the hospital. He wished me well and hoped I would be discharged from the hospital soon.

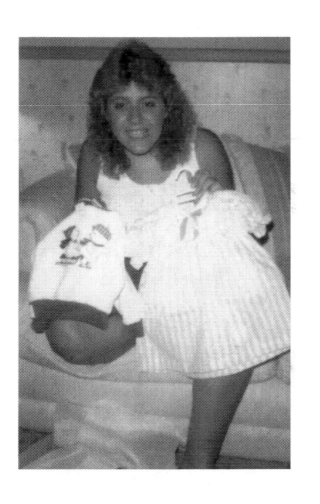

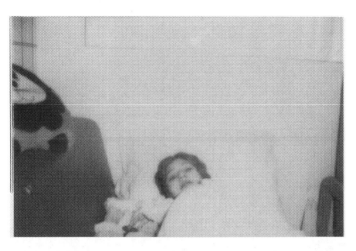

Chapter Twelve

Week seven, my sister's wedding was one week away and I was still in the hospital! The doctors said I would be discharged by her wedding but with the way things were going I did not think that was going to happen. By Thursday of that week, however, we were told that as long as my blood counts looked good I could be discharged on Saturday (the day before her wedding!). I was so happy to hear that. I was finally going home!!!!

For the most part I stayed in my room because I did not want to take a chance of getting another infection and stop me from getting out of the hospital. When Friday came I found out I was getting another four hour pass to go to my home to spend some time with family and out-of-town guests who were attending the wedding. (A Greek tradition is to have a "three day" celebration. Celebrate with family and friends on Friday evening and Saturday evening and then at the wedding is on Sunday).

I was really happy to get out again, for a few hours, and spend time with relatives I had not seen in a long time.

Everyone was asking me how I felt and told me I was in their thoughts and prayers. When it was time to take me back to the hospital, my cousin Chris offered to drive me back since my parents had a house full of guests. My parents told her that would be a great help. I was glad to spend some extra time with my cousin Chris. And, my cousins from Michigan, Jimmy and Mary were coming along. I had not seen them in a while so I was very happy that they were coming too!

I got back to the hospital and informed the nurses I was back in my room. My cousin Chris helped me get my pajamas on, wash my face and "clean" my teeth/mouth with the peroxide & sterile water solution. My nurse came in and got the IV hooked back up and said my cousins could stay for a little while. I was glad that they could because I really did not want to be alone. I hated leaving my house with all my family there. I think my cousins could tell I was a little depressed about having to leave. They also knew that I was not going to enjoy my sister's wedding as much since I did not feel that good.

To make me feel better they started telling jokes and talking about funny stuff to help me feel better. I knew we were laughing a lot but did not realize how loud until my nurse came into the room and said we had to quiet down. She also said my cousins could only stay a few more minutes because it was getting late. Even though I did not want them to go I knew they had to. They hugged me and told me good-bye and that they would see me tomorrow. I thanked them for driving me back to the hospital and for making me laugh. I really needed some "laughs".

When I got into bed I felt tired but I did not sleep very well. I think I was too excited to sleep because I was finally getting out of the hospital!! Even though the nurses and doctors took wonderful care of me and I was going to miss them, after seven weeks in the hospital, I was ready to go home!! Since I did not sleep well, I was up early that morning. My nurse came into my room to take my vital signs one last time and remove the IV from my hand before discharging me. I told her "PLEASE take the IV out of my hand so I can GO HOME!!!!"

Still having the concern of the anemia and bleeding precautions, she bandaged my hand well after removing the IV. Finally, free of any tubing, I tried to wash myself up as well as I could. I had to wait until Ellen came to get dressed because I felt too weak. I did not want to take a chance of falling while getting dressed. Again, since my parents had out-of-town guests staying at the house, my cousins came with my sister to help take me home. They helped me finish getting ready and eat some breakfast. Then they packed up all my things, which took a while. After being in the hospital for seven weeks, I had accumulated a lot of stuff!

While packing things up, Dr. Jerry came and gave Ellen the official discharge papers and instructions. He told my sister that I needed to return to the hospital in four days to the outpatient Hematology/Oncology clinic for my first visit. I would receive instructions on my chemotherapy treatment plan, for the post induction phase, at that time. Ellen and I told him we understood all of the instructions, and we would let Mom and Dad know all the information once we were home. Finally it was time to leave. I was a little sad when I was saying "good-bye" to the nurses, doctors and the other patients on the floor, but I was ready to go home!!!

Chapter Thirteen

Despite my desire to get home, being there felt "weird". I did not know why, but the house seemed different to me. My mom and dad and everyone else that was at our house gave me a hug and welcomed me back. My mom thought I looked a little tired so she told me to go lie down for a while. This way I would be rested up for when more company arrived later. With not sleeping so well the night before, taking a nap sounded good. I went upstairs to my room and laid down on my bed!!!

Being back in my room felt really good. It did not take long for me to fall asleep. After a couple of hours, my mom came and woke me up. She asked how I was feeling and I told her I felt okay. I told my mom I was ready to get up and eat a little something since it was lunchtime. My mom made me some soup and a grilled cheese sandwich, hoping this meal would be easy for me to eat. I tried my best, but with the mouth ulcers it was not easy. I could tell my mom was upset watching me eat because she knew I was in pain. She told me to take my time and to take small bites so it would not hurt as much. It took over an hour, but I did finish my lunch!

By early evening guests were arriving at our house. Once again I got to be with relatives I had not seen in a while. They were asking me how I was feeling and about being diagnosed with Leukemia. The rest of the night went quick and I was tired. Even though a few guests were still at our house, I told my mom and dad I was going to bed. I said "goodnight" to everyone and kissed my mom and dad before going up to my room. Even though I was tired, it took me a while to fall asleep. It was so different from being the hospital. My room was so quiet. Also, I tossed and turned most the night because I was excited about the wedding.

Morning came and even though I did not get much sleep, I felt good. It was Ellen's wedding day and I had been excited about this day for a very long time!! We all had a quick breakfast together and then little by little we started getting ready. I was excited to get my bride's maid dress on and to see Ellen in her wedding dress. She had a beautiful dress and veil, and I knew she would look very pretty in it. Before I knew it, the time had come for us to leave for the church.

When we arrived, we entered the chapel. It looked beautiful with all the wedding decorations. I sat down in one of the pews with my brother Jimmy, while my parents and Ellen were taking care of things before the wedding ceremony. Jimmy was a year younger than me. Since we were so close in age, we fought all the time and got on each other's nerves. But, I did miss him after being in the hospital for seven weeks. I told Jimmy I loved him and I missed him. I also told him sorry for Mom and Dad having to spend so much time away from home. He said he loved and missed me too and it was okay that mom and dad had to be at the hospital. He said he just wanted me to get better and that he would try not to fight with me so much. I told him that I would try too not to argue with him so much either.

After my mom and dad returned to the chapel, we went into the bridal room while the guests were arriving. Chris, Souli and other family and friends that were part the wedding party also arrived and joined us. They said I looked very pretty. I told them I was not happy about wearing a wig. But, at least I was out of the hospital and able to attend my sister's wedding!!

I was nervous going down the aisle in front of everyone, but overall I felt good. During the ceremony my mom and dad waved to me to come and sit down but I was okay standing. I guess being up at the alter watching my sister get married, I forgot I was sick. After the ceremony was finished I was tired and needed to sit down. I was able to sit for a while during all of the "after wedding" pictures. Then once again we got into our vehicles and drove to the reception hall.

The hall was decorated just as beautiful as the church. The food looked and smelled good but I was not able to enjoy it very much because of the mouth ulcers. My mom asked me if I was able to eat anything and I told her I ate the best that I could with the sores and all. Dinner was done and it was time for the dancing.

There are several traditional Greek dances that are done at the beginning of the "Greek Dancing". I was able to dance to a few songs and then I began to feel the tiredness/fatigue. I told Mom and Dad I was going to sit down for a little bit and then try to dance some more. There were lots of people out on the dance floor having fun and I wanted to be out there with them, but I just did not have the energy.

Several of my relatives asked me how I was feeling. I told them I would rather be out on the dance floor than sitting in the chair, but I had to listen to my body. Dr. Jerry told me before I was discharged that I needed to be careful while at the wedding. He said, "I know it's your sister's wedding but you have to be careful. You don't want to be readmitted into the hospital do you?" So as much as I wanted to be dancing with Ellen and everyone else, I did what I was told and just watched. Overall I had a great time!

The night passed too quickly and before I knew it the reception was ending. The celebration lasted until the hall closed. I wouldn't say that the hall employees were kicking us out, but they did have to remind us a couple of times that we needed to "wrap things up". Little by little they got the gifts and other stuff packed up in the cars. My mom and dad did not want me to help. They told me to keep sitting and relax. Several family members helped out so it did not take too long. I was really tired by the end of the night and ready to go home.

Once there, all I wanted to do was go to bed. As much as I loved wearing my dress, I was ready to take it off and get into my comfy pajamas. I hugged and kissed my family good-night and went to bed. For the first time in weeks I slept through the night.

Chapter Fourteen

Four days went by fast. It came time for my appointment at the outpatient Hematology/Oncology clinic. Dad drove me to the hospital. This became a regular drive for the two of us during the next three years.

When we arrived, the receptionist already knew me since I had been in the clinic several times before for my bone marrow aspiration and spinal tap tests. While we signed in, I introduced her to my dad. Before I could sit down in the waiting room, I needed to have blood drawn for lab work and to get my height and weight taken. We did not sit in the waiting area too long before we were put in a room.

The nurse entered the room and introduced herself to us. I did not recognize her from previous visits to the clinic. She asked me how I was feeling and looked me over. When she was done, she said my doctor would be in shortly.

A few minutes later Dr. Jerry entered the room (I knew he would be my physician at the outpatient clinic). He had some papers and prescriptions in his hands. The first thing he wanted to go over with us was the plan for my post induction chemotherapy treatments. He gave my dad the prescriptions and went over each medication with us. This was the plan he thought would be best for me for the next two or more years (but, could be changed depending how I responded to the treatment):

1. 6-mercaptopurine oral pills taken every day
2. Bactrim oral pills taken every day
3. Methotrexate oral pills taken once a week (every Friday)
4. Prednisone oral pills taken for seven days each month (usually the last week of the month)
5. Vincristine given via IV once a month
6. Ten treatments of radiation to the head (to be given in the next two weeks)

Dr. Jerry gave us information pamphlets on the chemotherapy drugs and the side effects. He also gave me directions on how and when the medications should be taken. He told my dad he needed to get the prescriptions filled that day at the hospital pharmacy so I could start taking the medications the following day.

He also went over the plan for my regular outpatient Hematology/Oncology visits, bone marrow aspirations and spinal taps. He stated that I would come to the clinic once a week for about two months, then the visits would space out to every other week for about two months and then once a month for the next two years (until I was done with chemotherapy treatments). My dad and I knew for the next few years there would be a lot of visits to the hospital, the information was still overwhelming. My doctor also said he was going to get the radiation treatments scheduled so when I returned the following week he would have the exact dates.

After about three hours at the outpatient clinic it was finally time to leave. My dad scheduled the next appointment, then, we went to the pharmacy to get my chemotherapy prescriptions filled. Once the prescriptions were filled, my dad was in shock on what he owed for the medications. He asked the pharmacist "I have insurance, did they not cover these medicines?" The pharmacist responded "yes sir, we did bill your insurance, however, this is the amount that was left over." Even though we had insurance, my medications were very expensive. My parents would have to pay a lot of money out of their own pocket!

Once we reached home, my dad told me to put the medications in a safe place but one where I would not forget to take them. "You know how important it is to take these medications like your doctor told you," he said. "If you start to feel sick after taking them make sure you let me and your mom know. From now on you have to tell us how you feel so if there is anything serious we can let your doctor know, okay."

The next day, after eating breakfast, I took my medications as ordered. I thought to myself "for the next two years or so this will be my daily routine." I was very good about taking my medications as ordered. It got to be where any time I knew I was leaving the house for more than just a couple of hours I would take my pills with me.

At my next clinic appointment, Dr. Jerry told us he had scheduled my radiation treatment for the following week. My dad was going to have to take me to University Hospital for the radiation treatments since Children's hospital did not perform those treatments. University Hospital was just down the street from Children's. I would receive ten radiation treatments, one treatment every day for ten days in a row. I asked my doctor if this type of treatment hurt, he told me "no". I was just hoping he was right and that this did not hurt too much.

When we arrived at University Hospital, we got a little lost trying to find the Outpatient Radiology department. We finally found a hospital employee that was able to direct us to where we needed to go. Once we found the right area, we signed in and the receptionist took the information that she needed and told us the doctor would be with us shortly. I got those butterflies in my stomach again because I did not know what the radiation treatment would be like. Even though I was told the treatment would not hurt, I still did not believe it.

We did not have to wait long before a doctor came into the waiting area and called my name. He introduced himself and told us to follow him to one of the exam rooms. The doctor went over the information he had already received about me, then, asked some more questions. He went over the radiation treatment Dr. Jerry had ordered for me. I was to receive three minutes of radiation to both the right and left side of my head. In a few minutes I would go to the treatment area so the radiation techs could put the "marks" on my head for the radiation treatments.

He asked me if I had any questions. I asked, again, if the treatment would hurt. He told me "no", but, I might have a headache after receiving a radiation treatment. After he obtained all the information he needed, he took us down to the treatment area. We were greeted by a radiology tech and she told us to follow her into the treatment room. She had a measuring tape and a marker in her hand. She seemed nice and was very talkative with us.

Before we started she asked, "I need you to remove your wig." I took my wig off and handed it to my dad to hold on to while she was measuring my head and putting bright red marks on it. She told me to be very careful while I was showering not to wash the marks off. They needed to stay on until I was done with the radiation treatments. She told me "you don't want to go through all this again, so be careful."

The room was big and there were other radiation machines in there that would be used for other parts of the body. I still had the butterflies in my stomach because I was not 100% convinced that this treatment was pain free. I guess I would find out in a couple of days. Before leaving, the tech looked at the treatment schedule. The tech asked my dad, "Would you like Anastasia to have morning or afternoon appointments?" My dad asked if they had afternoon appointments available since it would be easier to leave work towards at that time. She stated there was and scheduled me for 3:00pm appointments. "Okay, you are all set, see you on Monday" she said.

Monday arrived and I felt the "fear of the unknown" again. Even though I had seen the radiation room and equipment, I still was worried. Once there, we entered the waiting room and I signed in. A few other patients sat in the room, all of them much older than me. We were sitting close to a woman who, I thought, looked to be in her sixties. She started talking to us. I told her I was very nervous about receiving my first radiation treatment. She told me not to worry. She stated the treatment itself was painless, "you just have to make sure you stay still during the treatment." Talking to her did help me relax since I was getting the information from someone who actually had a treatment and not a doctor who had not.

While we were talking, her name was called. "I'll see you tomorrow, she said, I have at least two more weeks to go." My dad and I answered "okay, see you tomorrow." Only a few more minutes passed and my name was called. I stood up and followed the tech into the room I had been in before. She told me to take my wig off and set it on the table in the corner. Then she had me lay on the table that was under the radiation machine. The tech was glad to see that the red marks that were drawn on my head had not been washed off. I told her I was very careful when showering not to rub them off.

"Lay on your right side first," she said. Using masking tape, she gently taped my head to the table to keep it from moving during the radiation. Before she left the room she told me the treatment would take about three minutes and to make sure I stayed still. "There are speakers in the room," she said. "I'll let you know when the radiation starts and when it is finished. If you need anything, talk loudly, I'll be able to hear you. Are you ready?" "I guess," I said reluctantly.

She walked out the door and within a few seconds I heard her voice over the speaker system. "Okay, your treatment is about to begin. Remember to stay still." Even though I did not look up, I knew when the treatment started because a bright light was on the sheet that I was laying on. I felt the butterflies in my stomach again because I thought for sure there would be some kind of pain. I could hear radio music playing softly in the room which helped the time pass by. Before I knew it the tech spoke into the speaker and said the treatment for the right side of my head was done.

The tech re-entered the room and got me repositioned for the left side of my head. Now, knowing the treatment was not bad, I let myself relax and just listen to the music. The three minutes went by quickly and the tech re-entered the room again. She helped me off the table and put my wig back on. As I was walking out towards the waiting room she waved. "See you tomorrow," she said.

When I entered the waiting room, I could tell my dad had a worried look on his face. He was not sure, like me, if I had experienced any pain during the treatments. He had seen me go through enough pain up to now. The last thing he wanted to hear was that I had experienced more. "I'm okay Dad," I told him. "The radiation did not hurt." I could see the look of "relief" on his face once I told him I was fine. He hugged me and said "Well one down, nine more treatments to go. You think you can handle that?" "Yes," I said. I was thinking, the radiation treatments I can handle, it's the next two or more years of chemotherapy and all of the other tests that I'm not so sure about!

The ten days of radiation treatments went by quickly and went well. I did get some headaches afterwards as the doctor said I might, but they went away after taking some Tylenol. When the treatments were over, I was glad to finally wash the red marks off my head.

Chapter Fifteen

My radiation treatments finished on a Friday and the following Wednesday was my next clinic appointment. I was scheduled to have the first bone marrow aspiration and spinal tap done as an outpatient. My dad and I arrived at the clinic as usual. My blood was drawn, I was seen by my nurse and doctor and then it was time for the dreaded tests. Even though I had numerous bone marrow and spinal taps done, they were never something I got used to.

Up to now, my parents had never been in the treatment room with me during these procedures. I asked my dad if he would come in the treatment room with me this time, so I could hold his hand. "Okay," he said, and followed me and the nurses into the treatment room.

I knew the routine of lying on my stomach so they could clean the area first, then inject the numbing medicine. My dad was doing okay with this, even though I was really squeezing his hand because of the numbing medicine. It was when the nurse pulled out the big needle, which I had never seen, and pushed it into my lower back that made him feel queasy. He did not say anything, he just tried to tuff it out because he wanted to be there for me.

After the bone marrow aspiration was done, the nurses could tell my dad looked pale. "Mr. Nitsis, are you alright?" one of the nurses asked. "No I'm not," he said. "I am so sorry honey, but I can't be in here with you. I know you wanted to hold my hand, but I can't watch them poke you with those big needles." I told my dad that it was alright for him to leave the room. I could tell my dad felt bad for needing to leave. I assured him I would be okay. After he left the room, I was repositioned for the spinal tap (on my side with my knees as close to my head as I could get them). Once again, the fun began.

When the tests were done, I came out of the treatment room and my dad apologized again for not being able to stay in the room with me. I told him I completely understood because I did not think I could watch big needles being poked into someone's back either.

For the next three months my clinic visits were every two weeks. At the end of June (1983), during one of my clinic visits, my nurse told us about a camp for kids with cancer. This would be the first year for the cancer camp, in the Cincinnati area, and it was scheduled for a week in August. She stated the camp was for five days and all expenses were paid by the American Cancer Society so there would be no cost to us if I attended. She told us it would be a good experience for me. A nurse would be there the entire time to help with medications or any emergencies.

A feeling of fear came over me. I had never been camping before. Nor, had I been on a "vacation" without my parents. I did not feel comfortable about camping somewhere for five days without my mom or dad. It had only been one month since I was discharged from the hospital, so I was very reluctant about going to camp.

"I really think you will have fun at this camp," my nurse said. "You'll get to meet other children with cancer who are experiencing things you are right now." Even though I really did not want to go to camp, my dad told my nurse, "Go ahead and sign her up. I think it's a good idea too."

I thought to myself, "You two are crazy thinking this would be good for me." I had so many complications while I was in the hospital, so what if something went wrong while I was at camp. My nurse assured us several times that a nurse would be there the whole time. Even though I did not want to go, I was signed up for camp.

Chapter Sixteen

It was the beginning of July (1983). I had been home from the hospital for over a month. Even though I was home, things did not feel "normal". They would not for a long time. I had to get used to taking pills every day, I felt tired, my mouth was still healing from the ulcers and I had frequent hospital visits. I did not know if I would be healthy enough to attend school in September. My friends and my cousins would come over to visit me, which really made me happy. I did not leave my house too often since I tired so easily. Having family and friends come over to visit me helped bring some kind of "normal" back into my life and I was still very excited about becoming an aunt soon.

In the beginning of August (1983), I went to my scheduled clinic visit. I was feeling okay, but, my blood results indicated differently. Some of my counts were low so I was told not to take the Methotrexate for that week. I was to return to the clinic in one week and have my blood counts checked again. Three days later, my dad took me to the emergency room. It was a Saturday and the clinic was not open, so he had to take me to the ER. I had a fever, nausea, vomiting. My oncology doctor was contacted and I did not have to be admitted into the hospital. The ER doctor told me to continue to take Tylenol for the fever, drink plenty of fluids and rest. I was to go back to the hematology/oncology clinic on Wednesday as scheduled.

August 10, 1983. Back at the clinic for check-up and blood work. I was feeling better. The fever, nausea, and vomiting I had were gone. Next week was the camp for kids with cancer. I thought for sure since I was ill a few days prior that I would be told I should not go, but that was not the case. My blood counts looked better. I was told as long as I did not have any fevers, I could go to camp as planned. "Great," I thought, "I guess I'm not getting out of going to camp."

The camp I attended went from Saturday to Wednesday. When Saturday morning arrived, I had the butterflies in my stomach again. I had never been camping before so I wasn't sure what to expect. I knew we were staying in cottages and we would be sleeping in bunk beds but I did not know much more than that.

My parents helped me get the car packed up with my sleeping bag, blanket, pillow, clothes, toiletries, chemo meds, and other stuff. My dad and my brother Jimmy were the ones taking me to camp since my mom and my sister had to work. We were on the road around 9:00am in order to arrive on time for check-in. We had about a 45 minute ride and my dad could tell I was nervous about going. "Don't be so nervous honey," he told me, "You will be okay. It will be good for you to meet other kids with cancer."

When we pulled up to the camp entrance, there were signs directing us to the main building. A few other campers had also arrived. We went to the sign-in table and gave the camp staff the information they needed and then we were introduced to the nurse who was going to be there. My dad gave her my chemo meds and told her I knew when to take them and how much to take (some of the other children attending were younger than me and needed help with taking their medications). The nurse told my dad I was in good hands and not to worry. We were introduced to the rest of the camp staff and directed towards the girls' rooms. I picked out what bed I wanted to sleep on and put my sleeping bag on it. My dad and Jimmy helped me get the rest of my things out of the car and into the room I was in.

My dad encouraged me to talk to the other girls that were there and get to know a little about them. I had no problem talking to them. It was as if we had known each other for a while. This made me feel much better, and I thought I just might have a good time. My dad and Jimmy stayed for a little longer, but knew I was going to be okay if they left. They hugged and kissed me good-bye and told me to have a good time.

This first year, there were nine girls and nine boys that attended camp. Even though the ages of the campers ranged from about 5 to 14 years old, we all got along well and had a good time together.

We did lots of fun activities: swimming, nature hikes, horseback riding, arts & crafts, visited historical places near the camp, played games, listened to music, watched movies, night swims, and just some good old relaxation under the shade trees. The nurse that attended the camp was very caring and friendly. She enjoyed being there with us and participating in all the different activities. The camp staff was also very friendly, helpful and funny too. They had me laughing all the time!

I was surprised at how much energy I had, that I did not get tired too easily. I don't know if because my spirits were high, I felt less tired. I never thought I would have enjoyed camp as much as I did. I guess being able to talk to other kids with cancer really helped me. I did not feel "weird" around them, I could be myself. If I did not want to wear my wig, I did not have to. I was not worried about being starred at because of my bald head.

The five days of camp went quickly, we were all sad to have to say good-bye to each other. We wrote down each other's address so we could keep in touch with each other (which we did). We hugged each other good-bye as we fought back tears saying "see you next summer".

My dad and Jimmy came again to pick me up. On the ride home they asked me how everything went. I told them how much fun I had and all the activities we did and things we learned. I did not shut up the entire ride home! My dad was very glad I had so much fun. He had not seen me that happy in a long time.

Once home, Dad helped me unpack my things. "I haven't seen you this happy since you've been diagnosed," he told me. Going to camp really helped me be "myself" again and lifted a lot of the depression I felt after being diagnosed with Leukemia. I was really glad my dad signed me up for camp, it was a great experience for me!

I noticed I had more energy and I was more willing to go places again. After I was diagnosed I did not leave my home much. I did not feel like going anywhere. My cousins Chris and Souli and my friends would have to come to my house to visit me. This was not like me. I was always spending time over my aunt's house or at a friend's.

My next clinic visit, on August 23rd ('83), my nurse and the other clinic staff were anxious to hear how camp went. I told them how much fun I had and that I really enjoyed going and could not wait until next year to go again. I told them that meeting other kids with cancer, really helped me talk about things I wasn't able to talk to other people about. Also, I did not worry about others staring at me because I looked different, all I had to worry about was having fun. My nurse and the other staff were glad to hear I had such a good time and they, too, stated I seemed to be happier.

During this visit I had my routine blood work and "check-up" done, all looked good. I was also told, my hospital visits would be every month now, instead of every two weeks. This would change, however, if my blood counts went down or I became ill.

Chapter Seventeen

Summer had come to an end, and now, it was time to go back to school. This year, instead of being afraid of starting at a different school, I was afraid of starting school as a different "me". It had been five months since I last attended school and only a few of my friends had seen me over the summer. My principal, office staff and my teachers had been informed of my returning back to school. They were given information about my chemotherapy and that I would be leaving school early on a frequent basis to go to my hospital visits. They were also told that my immune system was not 100% due to the chemotherapy so, if I did not feel well, it was okay for me to go to the office and contact my parents.

The first day back to school went better than I thought. My friends that I had not seen in a long time, were glad to see me back. "How do you like my wig?" I asked them. They said they liked it and it looked like my own hair. They were asking me a lot of questions but I had to wait until lunchtime to tell them all that was going on. Teachers from the previous year, who saw me pass through hallways, welcomed me back. They told me I looked "good" and wished me the best. It took a couple of weeks for me to get used to being back to school but overall things went well.

October arrived and I was very excited because my sister was due to give birth anytime. The morning my niece Miranda was born, I was getting ready for school. I was in the kitchen when the phone rang. I wondered who would be calling that early in the morning, not thinking it would be my sister. I answered the phone and it was Ellen. I said "hello" and she asked me in a calm voice "what are you doing?" I told her I was getting ready for school and asked why she was calling so early in the morning. She tells me, again in a calm voice, "Oh, I just wanted to let you know I had a baby girl during the night."

I was so excited I started screaming, "A baby girl! You had a baby girl!!" I was so happy I started to cry. Once I calmed down, I asked Ellen how the delivery went and how was she feeling. "The delivery went well," she told me, "I feel okay right now, just really tired." She said even though she was tired she wanted to call me before I left for school to let me know that I was "officially" an aunt!! I went to school, but I had a hard time staying focused. All I kept thinking about was going to see my sister and my newborn niece at the hosital. I was telling everyone at school my sister had her baby and how excited I was.

Before I knew it, the month of October was almost over, and it was time for Halloween again. I could not believe how much my life had changed in one year. On Halloween night, I went over to see Chris and Souli. I went over to hang out with them and help Souli and her friend dress up for trick or treating. Chris and Souli asked me if I planned to go trick or treat and I told them "no" since I did not have a costume to wear.

Souli and her friend decided to be "punk rockers" since that what was "in" at the time. I was helping Souli put green and purple spray paint in her hair. While I was doing this my wig was off. I usually had my wig off when I was around my cousins, since I felt so comfortable with them. Souli and I were "clowning around" and a bit of the spray paint got in my head. Chris and Souli looked at me and said "you would make the perfect punk rocker with your short hair."

At that time, my hair was only a half inch long. In the early eighties girls did not have short hair like mine unless you were a "punk rocker". Chris said she had some clothes she thought would look perfect as an outfit and some jewelry too. At first I was hesitant, I was not comfortable being out in public without my wig on. They convinced me with it being Halloween that I would look great. So, as if on a mission, they got me dressed in some "punk" clothes, put a lot of makeup on me, gave me some crazy jewelry and sprayed my hair green & purple.

When I looked in the mirror I could not believe I was looking at myself. They really had me "made up". Chris, Souli and her friend could not stop telling me how "cool" I looked. When it was time to leave to go trick or treating I started to became nervous. Even though it was Halloween, I was not comfortable going out in public with my wig off.

As we approached the first house, I was getting a lot of stares from other kids that were trick or treating. They were good stares, though. I was complimented on how good I looked. As I was getting candy from one house, the lady asked me how I was able to get my hair so short. "Chemotherapy," I responded.

Almost every house I went to, I was told I was the best "punk rocker" that came to their house. For the first time since I had lost my hair, I was glad it was short.

That night of trick or treating was one of the best nights I had in a long time. When we returned to my aunt's house, Chris wanted to take a picture of me in "costume". A week or so later Chris gave me the picture. It did not look like me at all! When showed my friends the picture, they did not believe it was me. That was definitely one Halloween I would never forget!

November came, and little by little, I was trying to feel "normal" again. For the most part, I was doing well in my classes and with my homework. Some days I felt more tired than others. My teachers knew I was on chemotherapy, so if I told them I was not feeling well they understood. If I was unable to get an assignment done in class, they let me take it home and bring it back the next day. Even with being sick, I tried to do the best I could. When I had my monthly hospital visit for November, I felt good and my blood counts were normal. Also, I was told I gained some weight back (of the twenty pounds I had lost when I was first diagnosed).

Soon December was here and I was looking forward to Christmas coming. My sister and I took Miranda to a few malls to go shopping and see all the decorations. We also wanted to get a picture of Miranda with Santa Claus for her first Christmas. Even though she was only a few weeks old, Ellen and I had fun taking her to different places. I really loved becoming an aunt and enjoyed babysitting whenever asked. If a couple of days went by and I did not see Ellen and Miranda, I was calling Ellen to find out when they were coming over because I missed them! Spending time with my sister and niece made me happy and they kept my spirits up when I was not feeling very well.

My monthly clinic visit for December went well except for having a bone marrow aspiration and spinal tap done. The test results showed I was still in remission!!! My routine check-up was good and my blood counts were still normal, so I was told to continue with my chemo regimen. I had also gained a couple more pounds, consuming that wonderful Thanksgiving meal!

Chapter Eighteen

January 1984. Just after New Year's I went to my monthly clinic visit. Even though I felt okay, my blood work indicated otherwise. My doctor decreased my chemo amounts. I was told to come back to the clinic in one week to have my blood counts checked again. I went back to the clinic every week for six weeks to have my blood counts checked. Finally, at the end of February, I was put back on my chemo regimen 100%.

At the beginning of March, Ellen and I had taken Miranda over to my aunt's house to visit with her and Chris and Souli. My hair was about 1 ½ inches long now, so the wig was really getting itchy whenever I wore it. While at my aunt's, I took my wig of like I always did when I was over there. Ellen and my cousins were commenting how good my hair was growing in.

"Soula, your hair is coming in so pretty," said Chris and Souli. "It is, I don't think she needs to wear her wig anymore," responded Ellen. "Yeah," my cousins agreed. I, however, was not in agreement with them. "You guys are crazy," I told them, "Everyone will be staring at me. My hair is not long enough yet!" They continued to talk to me about it and got my confidence up. "I'll think about not wearing my wig, but, I'm really scared about people looking at me like I'm some kind of freak!" They told me not to listen to what people might say. I should not wear the wig anymore if it was itchy and uncomfortable.

A week or so later I had my monthly hospital appointment. I told my nurse about how my family had been trying to talk me into taking off my wig for good. She asked if I would take my wig off so she could see my hair. She too, agreed my hair looked very good even though it was short. She also said it might even help my own hair grown faster, if I no longer wore a wig. I was the one, however, that needed to make that decision. I should not be forced into it.

That week, while at school, I told some of my friends about not wearing a wig anymore. We went into the girl's bathroom when I knew that no one else was in there. I took off the wig so they could see my hair. They thought my hair looked good. But like me, they seemed a little hesitant about the idea of no longer wearing a wig. They knew being in Junior High, I would get some kind of teasing with such short hair. They told me whatever I decided to do they would be there to support me. The weekend was approaching, so I told them I was going make a decision during that time. I would either arrive Monday morning at school with a wig on or my own hair.

On Sunday evening, I decided I was going to go to school the next day without the wig on. I told my mom and dad, Ellen and Jimmy about my decision. My parents and my sister were excited for me, but my brother was more hesitant. Jimmy was a year younger than me so he attended Junior High also. He knew how bad kids teased each other and did not want me to get my feelings hurt. My family told me if I did get teased to not let it bother me and just continue to focus on my classes and school work. I told them I would try my best. I did wash and brush my wig just in case I changed my mind in the morning.

When I woke up Monday morning I did not feel so good. Not so much as I was sick, but that I was very nervous about my decision. I knew it was mine to make, no one had forced me. One day, sooner or later, I would have to go to school without the wig. So, I thought, "I might as well get it over with now."

As I got ready for school, the pit in my stomach was getting worse. I could barely eat my breakfast. When the time came for me to leave the house, I said to myself, "Here I go, there is no turning back now."

While waiting for the bus to arrive, I felt like every car that passed was staring at me. This was definitely going to be one of the hardest things I would have to deal with at school. The bus arrived. As I was walking onto the bus my stomach felt even worse. As I went to sit down, everyone on the bus WAS staring at me. Even though no one said anything, I could tell they were wondering why I had such short hair?"

Luckily, one of my good friends got on the bus at the next stop. I was so glad to have someone to talk to and not feel so strange. She sat down next to me and told me my hair looked good. "Yeah, it is a little short," she said, "But I think you look cute with short hair. Anyway, before you know it your hair will be long again." I was glad she was on the bus with me. She made me feel much better. When we arrived at school, she told me, "Don't listen to anyone if they tease you. Just walk away and don't let it bother you, okay!" "I'll try," I said.

Sure enough, as soon as I entered the school building, students and teachers that did not know me were staring. I was asked many, many times "Why is your hair so short?" I told them, "I have cancer and I am on chemotherapy, which made my hair fall out." For some, my response made them sympathetic. For others, they did not care and continued to tease me. I tried my hardest to not let it get to me.

By lunch, however, I could not deal with all these kids making fun of me anymore. I went to the office and told the staff wanted to call my dad. While talking to him on the phone, I started to cry. I told him I was not feeling well and asked him if he could pick me up. He asked if I needed to go to the hospital. I told him I did not feel that bad, I just wanted to go home and lie down for a while. He said he would pick me up shortly.

When my dad arrived, I got in the car and started to cry. I told my dad what a bad day I had, having to deal with all the staring and teasing. I told him I was no going back to school. "From now on I want to be home schooled," I said. My dad understood that I was going through a difficult time, but, staying home from school was not the answer. "I'll take you home right now so you can calm down and feel better. After today though, you are going back to school," he said sternly. I continued to argue that I was not going back to school, but, I did not win that fight.

The next day, I dreaded getting ready for school. I knew what lie ahead, but realized that my parents would not let me stay at home. As expected, the teasing continued. I just tried my best not to let it get to me. At times, I did get really frustrated and had to go into the bathroom to have a quick cry and "let it out." Each day I went back to school, it got a little easier. It took over a month, however, before EVERYONE at school finally left me alone!!

My next two monthly hospital visits (February and March '84) went fine with my routine bone marrow and spinal tap done on the March visit. All my labs looked good, and I was told to continue with my regular chemo schedule. April and May '84, however, did not go as well.

Just before my scheduled hospital visit for April, I started with a low grade fever, my throat was sore and I felt tired. My dad took me to hospital and I had blood work done as usual. My blood counts were down. The test results revealed I had a throat infection. I was put on antibiotics and told not to take any of my chemo pills for one week. In one week, I returned to have blood work done again. My blood counts were still down and I was to remain off my chemo. I went back to the hospital four weeks in a row due low counts. Finally on the fourth week, May 16th, I was able to go back on chemo. Not feeling 100% during this time was not good. It was the end of the school year and I had a lot of tests to study for. Luckily, I made it through the last couple weeks of school and did well on most of my final exams.

During June, July and August '84, I went to my routine monthly hospital visits. A bone marrow aspiration and spinal tap were done in June showing I was still in remission!! All my blood counts were also good, so I continued taking my chemo as scheduled. The summer went well, spending time with my family and friends.

In August I went to camp for kids with cancer again. Had a great time, just like I did the previous year. There were some new campers that attended, but it did not take long for them to become "one of the gang." That was what I enjoyed about this camp. We all looked out for each other. If someone was having a hard time with an activity, we tried to help them out. We did not tease each other. We were all there just to have a good time and forget about having cancer for a few days. The same nurse attended camp too. We were all so glad to see her again. We were happy to see the camp staff too. There was some new staff, but they were all great!!

Camp went by too quick as it did before. Having to say goodbye to everyone the second year was even harder. We continued to hug each other many times before we HAD to leave. "We will see each other next year," we kept saying.

September 1984. I was starting my freshmen year in High School. I hoped, now that my hair had grown to a normal length, I would not get teased by students that did not know me. I did not, however, want to deal with starting a new school again. Trying to find my way around all over again, was not going to be fun.

My dad went with me to the High School orientation. We walked around to find my classrooms, cafeteria, gym, etc. Then we went to the school office. My dad wanted to meet the office staff and let them know I had Leukemia and that I was on chemotherapy. He informed them that I had monthly hospital appointments and would be leaving school early on those days. The office staff told my dad that would not be a problem. They just wanted him, on those days, to come to the office to pick me up. That way, they knew I was leaving with a parent and not skipping school.

The first day of school was crazy, as I expected it would be. Even though, I had walked the building the week before, I still got lost. As I met each new teacher, I let them know about my Leukemia diagnosis, and they all seemed concerned about me. They all made a comment about having to deal with cancer at such a young age. My teachers also stated it was okay for me to go to the office if I did not feel well.

As with Junior High, it took a week or so to get used to a new routine. I enjoyed making new friends again and experiencing different classes. During the months of September, October, November and December '84, my blood counts were good and I stayed on my chemo regimen. I don't know how my counts stayed up as busy as I was, trying to keep up with my classes, homework, and other assignments. I went to the hospital each month for my scheduled appointments (a bone marrow aspiration and spinal tap were done in September and December).

Chapter Nineteen

I should have known that my blood counts would not stay normal for too long. After the holidays, I went to my scheduled hospital visit in the first week of January '85. At this visit, my blood counts were down again. Once more, my chemo regimen was decreased. I had to go back to the hospital, five weeks in a row, to check my blood counts. Finally, on the fifth week, I was able to go back on my regular chemo regimen.

During this time, even though my blood counts were down and I felt tired, I continued to attend school every day and keep up with my school work. For the months of March and April, I went to my monthly hospital appointments and my blood counts were normal.

A few days before my scheduled hospital appointment for May, I woke up not feeling too good. It was a school day, I did not want to stay home. My teachers were giving information about final exams and I did not want to miss that. Feeling miserable, I got ready and went to school. By the third class, I knew I was not going to make it the rest of the day. I went to my teacher and told him I felt very ill. I asked if I could go to the office to contact my parents. Knowing I had cancer, he said "Okay, I hope you feel better soon." As quick as I could, I picked up my belongings and went to the office.

As I entered, the office staff could tell I was not feeling well. They saw me on a regular basis, and to them I looked pale. My temperature was taken and the thermometer showed I had a temp of 101F. By this time, my body aches were getting worse, and I was starting to feel short of breath. I called my parents and told them that I did not feel well and that I had a fever. My dad sounded very concerned and said he would be there shortly.

When my dad arrived, he could tell something was wrong. I felt so fatigued, I needed his help to walk to the car. Once inside the car, I started to cry. "What's wrong honey, do you feel that bad?" he asked. "Yes, I do" I said. "That's why I am crying. I feel like I did the day I was diagnosed. I am afraid I have relapsed and that the Leukemia is back!!" I could tell my dad was worried too, as he fought back tears hugging me. "It's going to be alright," he told me, "Let's get you to the hospital and find out what's going on." I was only a couple of months away from being taken off chemo, for good!! I was afraid I had relapsed and would have to do the past two years all over again!!

We got to the hospital. My dad pulled up to the front door, instead of parking, since I was unable to walk very far. He helped me out of the car and into the clinic. He told me to sit down and wait for him while he parked. When we checked in, the receptionist saw that I was not feeling well. I was put in an exam room and just laid down on the exam table.

My nurse entered the room and asked how I was. I told her I felt horrible and I started to cry again. I told her I was afraid that my Leukemia had come back. She calmed me down and told me there could be many other reasons why I was sick. She took my temperature and it was higher than at school. She did a quick assessment, listened to my heart and lungs, and then went to get the doctor.

The two of them entered the room. "I hear you are feeling pretty rotten," said Dr. Jerry. "Yes, I do," I responded in a weak tone. He did his assessment, focusing on my breathing and lung sounds. "From what I am hearing, I think you have pneumonia," he said in a concerned voice. The fever, body aches, fatigue and shortness of breath all seemed to point to symptoms of pneumonia too. "You need to get a chest x-ray done to confirm that you have pneumonia. I am sending you to radiology right now to have that done," he said. Being told I had pneumonia was much better than finding out I had relapsed!!

I was taken to radiology for the chest X-ray. My dad stayed in the clinic so he could call my mom to give her what information he had at the moment. He told her not to worry and that he would call her back once he knew more. The X-ray techs were waiting for me when I arrived in radiology. In order to get good "pictures" of my lungs, I had to stand in certain positions. At times this was difficult for me since my body ached and I felt lethargic.

The X-ray results confirmed I had pneumonia. Dr. Jerry informed my dad and I that a lung biopsy needed to be done, in order to determine what type of pneumonia I had.

They wanted to obtain the lung sample surgically while I was put under anesthesia. This option would be less painful than just being given a local anesthetic where the biopsy would be performed. My dad was worried about me having surgery but agreed it was the better option.

Even though my doctor wanted the surgery done as soon as possible, I still had a fever. I could not have surgery until my temperature went down. I was given some Tylenol by suppository because my stomach needed to be empty. I was pretty nervous since I never had surgery before. I had been through a lot of procedures up to now, but not surgery.

I was sent to the OR prep area even though I still had a fever. A surgical team was waiting for me and my Dad as soon as we arrived. They all introduced themselves and then put me in an exam room. A couple of the OR nurses entered the room first to take my vital signs and ask some questions. There was important information they needed to know prior to me going into surgery. The surgeon then entered the room and went over the "specifics" of the surgery he was going to perform on me.

The surgeon was very nice, explained the surgery in terms that my dad and I could understand and answered all the questions we had. The entire surgical staff was very nice. They could tell I was very stressed about my first surgery and helped me get relaxed. After talking to the doctor my dad called my mom to give her all the information he had up to that point. My mom wanted to come to the hospital, but my dad told her to stay home. He told her it would be better for her to come to the hospital after I was out of surgery. That way my mom would be able to come with Ellen and Jimmy (Ellen was still at work and Jimmy was still at school). My mom was hesitant toward my dad but she agreed.

I was finally ready for surgery and I was wheeled into an operating room. All the surgical staff had their masks and gowns on. They asked me "how are you feeling?" "Very nervous," I replied. They told me everything would be "okay" and that it was time for them to give me the medicine that was going to put me to sleep. As the medicine was injected into my IV, I was told to start counting backwards from ten to one. I think I made it to number eight and that is all I remember.

My surgery went well and I was taken to the recovery room. It took me a couple of hours to wake up. I was so tired!! My parents kept trying to wake me up. I told them how tired I felt, but I needed to wake up so I could leave the recovery room. Little by little the "grogginess" started to wear off. Dr. Jerry from the Hematology/Oncology clinic came to see how I was doing. He told my parents I would be admitted into the ICU for a few days until my respiratory status improved.

Due to the pneumonia, I was in respiratory distress and needed to be on oxygen. Also, I had a chest tube that was inserted on the left side of my chest where the lung biopsy was done. In the ICU I could be watched more closely in case of an emergency. I finally woke up enough to be transported there. I was given some pain medicine in my IV while still in the recovery room. This way, I would not be in too much pain while being transported.

It was late evening by the time I was admitted into the ICU. My parents stayed as long as they could, but eventually it was time for them to go. They were not able to stay with me during the night in the ICU like they did when I was of floor 3-east. My parents kissed and hugged me and said "goodnight". "See you tomorrow," they told me. They had that worried look on their faces that I had seen before, but they knew the nurse would take good care of me. I slept okay the first night. I think it was because I was so worn out from such a long day.

Chapter Twenty

When I woke up the next morning I felt like I had been beaten up. I tried to reposition myself and my entire body hurt. I let out such a loud scream that my nurse came running to my bedside. She asked me what was wrong and I told her I was in a lot of pain when I tried to move. She tried to reposition me but it hurt too much. I could also feel the chest tube on my left side. For the next three days I suffered a lot of pain. I was given morphine, but it only dulled the pain. I dreaded having to be repositioned in bed, or even worse, being put on a bed pan!! My nurses always made sure I had a dose of pain medicine before trying to move me around. And they tried to move me slowly to help decrease the pain.

Little by little, I started to improve. The chest tube was taken out and I was taken off oxygen. I was in the ICU for seven days when my doctor decided I was well enough to be transferred to a regular room. My parents and I were told I was going to be transferred to floor 3-East since I had been on that floor before.

When it was time to transfer me, it took both my nurse and the patient transporter to get me from the bed into the wheelchair. After being in bed for an entire week, I had no strength or energy. Once I was all situated in the wheelchair, I was given the "okay" to go down to 3-East.

I had been back to floor 3-East a couple of times since I was first diagnosed to say "Hello" to my nurses who took care of me, but it had been a while since my last visit. Being back on that floor brought many memories, some good and some bad. I could not believe it when I was wheeled into the same room I had been admitted in two years ago!

The room had changed a little bit and repainted with some brighter colors, but it did not change the feelings that were overwhelming me. I could also see the expression on my parents' face, knowing they were feeling the same way I was. I experienced some very difficult times while in that room and they would not be forgotten. The nurses remembered my parents and me and said "Hi". They asked me how I was feeling. I told them I felt much better than I did a week ago. As we were talking, the nurses helped get me in bed and put my belongings away.

I had been in my room for a couple of hours when Dr. Jerry arrived. He wanted to see how I was feeling and do a quick "head to toe" assessment. When he was done, he showed me some breathing exercises to do to help strengthen my lungs. "Also," he told me, "I want you get out of bed and walk around at least three times a day. This will help get your muscle and lung strength back. Start out slow, then, try to go a little farther each day." "Okay, I will try my best," I told him.

Before Dr. Jerry left, my parents asked him how much longer I would be in the hospital. He told my parents I would be there at least one more week. "I want her on IV antibiotics for a full two weeks before being discharged. I don't want to take the chance the pneumonia coming back because she was discharged too early." I did not want to be in the hospital for one more week, but I knew Dr. Jerry was just doing what was best for me.

Since I was in a private room again, my parents were able to spend the night with me if they wanted to. I told them they did not have to, but they said they would feel better if they did. Dad said he would stay the night with me first. He thought since I was so weak, he would have an easier time helping me get out of bed verses my mom. She agreed.

The second week in the hospital was almost as hard as the first. I was not in as much pain, but trying to get my strength back took some work. When I first started to walk around, I did not get very far. Each time though, as my doctor told me, I tried to walk a little farther. Being so weak reminded me of when I was first diagnosed. Once again, I was very lucky to have all my family there to help motivate me and keep trying. The ICU had very strict rules so I did not have many visitors other than my immediate family.

At the end of the second week, my doctor thought I was doing well enough to be discharged. Even though I was going home, he wanted me to wait one more week before returning to school. Once again, I was missing the end of the school year except for the last few days. This was not fun because I had to take my final exams in two days instead of one week. I did the best I could even though I did not have much time to study while in the hospital. I was very glad when I found out I passed all my exams!

One week after my discharge, I had a follow up visit at the clinic. Dr. Jerry told me I needed to be very careful about being around people who were sick for the next few weeks. Even though I was doing better my immune system was still low and he did not want me to get pneumonia again.

A month had gone by and it was time for my July ('85) clinic visit. I was due for another bone marrow aspiration and spinal tap to be performed. Even though I had gone through those procedures numerous times, I was still nervous. This time, however, I was more nervous than usual. I was told (at my previous clinic visit) as long as my blood work, bone marrow and spinal fluid "looked good," I would be taken off chemo. I had been on chemotherapy for over 2 years and I was ready to be done with it.

While being examined, my nurse and Dr. Jerry commented on this being my last day on chemo (pending the test results) and told me how excited they were for me. They knew the hard journey I'd gone through to get to this point, and they were very happy for me. After my exam was done I was told I could go into the treatment room for my bone marrow aspiration and spinal tap. The nurses in the treatment room also congratulated me on possibly being taken off chemo. This visit took longer than usual since Dr. Jerry wanted to know the results of all the tests before my dad and I left. I could tell my dad was anxiously waiting for the results just like I was.

Finally, after a very long wait, Dr. Jerry returned to my exam room. "I am pleased with the results of your blood, bone marrow and spinal fluid," he stated, "You can go off the chemo pills at this time. For the next year, however, you still need to come to the clinic every month. We will continue to do monthly blood tests, and perform the bone marrow and spinal taps every three months for another year. As long as you stay in remission," he proceeded, "You will stay off of chemotherapy." I was reminded I still had three more years of hospital visits, blood work, bone marrow aspirations and spinal taps before being considered cured. Even though I had at least three more years of this "unknown journey ahead", I was so glad to be taken off chemo! As sick as I was when diagnosed, I never thought I would get to this point!!

I couldn't wait to get home to tell my mom, Ellen and Jimmy that I was off chemo! They knew how excited I was about it and they were very happy for me. Mom made my favorite meal, spaghetti and meatballs, for dinner. It tasted the best it had in a long time. Chemo always made food taste funny, even my favorite foods. We were all smiling and laughing more than usual during dinner. I just hoped the worst was behind me, that I remained in remission and then eventually be "cured of cancer"!!

Chapter Twenty-One

I started my sophomore year in high school in September ('85) and felt better than I had in a long time. I had more energy and was able to focus better on my school work. I continued to do well in the remaining months of '85, going to my monthly hospital visits in October, November and December. I had a bone marrow aspiration and spinal tap done in October which showed I was still in remission!

January of 1986 started well. I had been off chemo for six months so I felt better and no major illnesses other than the occasional cold symptoms. The results of the bone marrow aspiration and spinal tap done that month showed I was still in remission. I was doing well in school. I was having fun spending time with my family and friends. I always had a close relationship with my family but being diagnosed with cancer made that bond even closer, especially with my cousins Chris and Souli. I also found out I was going to be an aunt again! I was so happy when Ellen told me she was having another baby. I enjoyed being an aunt so much with Miranda I couldn't wait to have another niece or nephew!

I had my monthly hospital visits in February, March, April and May with a bone marrow aspiration and spinal tap done in April. I remained in remission. I finished my sophomore year and was glad for summer to arrive. I had my monthly hospital visits for June, July and August with bone marrow and spinal tap done in July showing I was still in remission!! I was always nervous waiting for the test results because even though I felt good, I was worried about the Leukemia coming back.

In August ('86) I went to camp again and could not wait to tell my friends I was still cancer free one year after going off chemo. There were other campers who had been diagnosed around the same time I was. They, too, had been off chemo for almost a year and still in remission, so we were all happy for each other. Over the last three years that we attended camp, some of our friends had passed away so staying in remission was a very big deal to all of us. I also could not wait to tell them my sister was having another baby! I had brought pictures of Miranda for them to see. I told them how much I enjoyed being an aunt and I was really going to miss her while I was away at camp.

As usual, the week at camp went by too quickly. On the day our parents were coming to pick us up I got a big surprise. Usually, my dad and my brother Jimmy would be the ones to pick me up from camp. This time, however, my mom, Ellen and Miranda came with them. I always talked a lot about all my friends at camp and how much fun we had together. So my whole family decided to pick me up so they could meet the other kids that changed my life so much and helped me get through the hard times of being diagnosed.

I introduced my family to all my friends and of course they all thought Miranda was really cute. She was almost three years old at that time and very adorable. We all had a good time. Then it was time to say "goodbye" to everyone which was always very hard. On the ride home, as usual, I talked the whole way about all the activities we did during the week. I could tell my family was happy for me. They knew this was one place I could be "myself" and not worry about people thinking I was "different."

In September ('86) I started my junior year of high school. Some of my classes were harder than the previous year but I still did okay. I felt good and had not had any major illnesses since being taken off chemo. My life was finally "normal" expect for the monthly hospital visits. In October ('86) I became an aunt again. My sister had another girl, named Melissa, and I was very happy to have two nieces now. I had lots of fun with Miranda, now I had two nieces to have fun with!! I think being an aunt really helped me keep my spirits up when I felt "down" and keep me fighting to stay alive!

I had my monthly hospital visits for September, October and November ('86). All my test results showed I was still in remission! At my December hospital visit Dr. Jerry told me since I had remained in remission for 18 months after being taken off chemo, my hospital visits would be every three months for the next year.

Chapter Twenty-Two

January 1987. Overall I was still doing well. At my January hospital visit my blood counts were down a little. I told Dr. Jerry I had a slight sore throat but otherwise I felt "okay". I was given antibiotics and told to come back to the hospital in two weeks just to have blood work done again. I returned to the hospital for the follow-up visit and my counts were back to normal. Even though my hospital visits were supposed to be every three months now, Dr. Jerry wanted me to return for another visit in March. At my March visit I was feeling well, my blood counts were good and I was still in remission. I was told to return in May ('87) for the next visit. At my May visit I continued to feel well and blood counts remained normal. I was told to return in August.

In June ('87) I finished my junior year of high school and was ready for summer break! My mom, my aunt Katina, Souli and I went to Greece for a few weeks to visit family. I had grandparents, aunts, uncles and cousins that lived in Greece. It had been over seven years since I had seen them. They were very worried about me when they heard I had cancer. Finally being able to see me four years after being diagnosed, they were glad to see that I was doing well. We had so much fun while we were there. Also, getting to spend every day with Souli during that time was great too.

In August we came back from Greece and had a couple of weeks left of summer. At my August hospital visit I was feeling well and my blood results were normal and my doctor stated he was very happy I doing well. I still had one more year before I would officially be considered "cured", but I hoped I remained in remission!! I was told to return in November for my next hospital visit.

In September ('87), I began my last year of high school. My friends and I were very happy to finally be seniors!! Even though this was my fourth year attending high school, it felt different starting the school year as a senior. My classes were a little tougher and it seemed like I had more homework to do, but I was able to keep up.

At my November hospital visit I told Dr. Jerry, my nurse and other hospital staff that my senior year was going well. My blood results for that visit were normal and showed I was still in remission! I was told my next scheduled visit would be in March ('88).

The holidays came and went too quick as usual, but having "little ones" around always made the holidays seem more fun. Miranda and Melissa were so cute, I was very glad to be an aunt! I was always showing my friends at school pictures of them. We rung in the New Year of 1988, and now I only had a few more months left of high school.

I went to my March hospital visit and my blood tests continued to show I was in remission! I was told my next visit would be in July ('88). The next few months went by very quickly. I could not believe I was finished with high school! I was happy and sad about graduating. I knew once school was over, I probably would not see a lot of the other students anymore. I was going to miss my teachers, too.

My high school had a big graduation ceremony in the Convention Center in downtown Cincinnati. There were many people who attended. Even wearing my cap and gown, I could not believe High School was over. Being overwhelmed with "life" in general over the last five years, I planned on taking a break from school and not attend college until January 1989.

Chapter Twenty-Three

In July ('88) I had my last scheduled hospital visit. It was hard to believe five years had passed! When I went to the lab to have blood drawn, I said "goodbye" to all the staff there. They told me how good I looked and how happy they were for me. They knew the tough journey I had experienced!

Once my blood results were in, Dr. Jerry and my nurse came into the exam room. They stated my blood counts were normal and congratulated me on being considered "cured"! My parents and I were very happy to hear those words!! "I made it!! It's been five long years, but I made it," I said, with tears in my eyes!! Then we all started to cry, including my doctor and nurse.

Dr. Jerry went over several things with us since it was my last visit. He stated even though I would not be returning to the Hematology/Oncology clinic, it was very important that I continue to see a doctor EVERY year for a checkup. I was considered "cured", but it did not mean the Leukemia would never come back. I was told each year I remained in remission after being "cured", the risk of the Leukemia coming back decreased.

In a way I was sad that this was my last appointment at the Hematology/Oncology clinic. I had spent a lot of time there. I was going to miss my doctor(s), nurse(s) and all the hospital staff I had seen the past five years. As we were leaving, all of the staff congratulated me again on being "cured" and wished me the best of luck.

On the way out, we passed through the treatment area where the other children were receiving their chemo treatments. I hoped that one day they, too, would be considered "cured". I knew all of them may not survive and that made me very sad. That day I made a promise to myself. As long as I was healthy and able to, I would raise money for cancer research.

To this day, I have kept that promise. Since being diagnosed, I have volunteered and participated in numerous benefits, walks, relays, marathons, etc. to raise money for several organizations that are involved in cancer research and cancer patient programs/assistance. It is also the reason I have written this book about my own experience. Proceeds of this book will go towards cancer research and programs for cancer patients.

Not only have I been diagnosed with cancer, but many of my family members and friends have been diagnosed with the disease as well. Some survived, however, too many did not and left this world so much earlier than they should have. Whether it is a child or an adult who dies, their death is very upsetting for their loved ones. So, I am hoping to raise money and assist in whatever way I can to help find a cure for cancer and SAVE MORE LIVES!!

Currently, I am healthy and doing well. Being diagnosed with cancer is the reason I chose to become a nurse. I am a pediatric nurse and work with children with developmental and behavioral disabilities.

I was not able to have children, however, I am very blessed to have my beautiful nieces Miranda and Melissa, my awesome nephews Corey and Nikolaos and my beautiful great-nieces Taylor, Nora, Chloe and Brooklyn. I love you all so much! Words cannot express how much you mean to me. I am very grateful that I am alive and able to be a part of your lives!!

Also, I want to thank all my family again for being there for me when I needed them the most!!! Even though it has been over 36 years since I was diagnosed, all the love and support you gave me will stay with me FOREVER!!! I love you and again, thank you, thank you, thank you!!!

04160802 00955781

Printed in the United States
By Bookmasters